LEATHERCRAFT

Traditional Handcrafted Leatherwork Skills and

LEATHERCRAFT

Traditional Handcrafted Leatherwork Skills and Projects

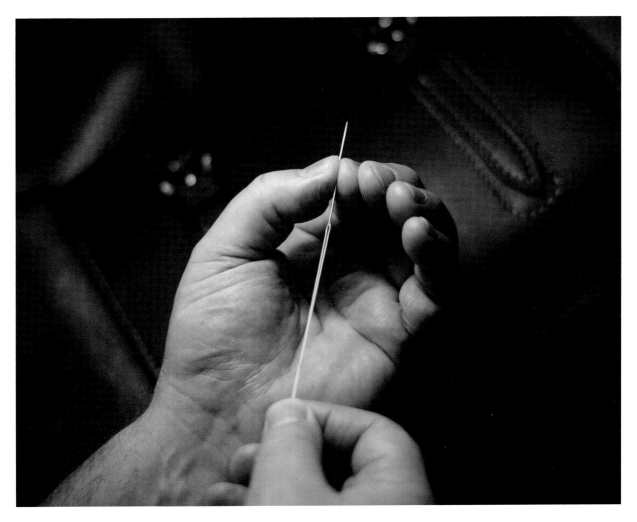

NIGEL ARMITAGE

SCHIFFER
PUBLISHING
4880 Lower Valley Road · Atglen, PA 19310

Produced by BlueRed Press Ltd. 2020
Interior design by Insight Design Concepts Ltd.
Type set in Bembo and Bliss

ISBN: 978-0-7643-6039-8
Printed in India

Published by Schiffer Publishing, Ltd.
4880 Lower Valley Road
Atglen, PA 19310
Phone: (610) 593-1777; Fax: (610) 593-2002
Email: Info@schifferbooks.com
Web: www.schifferbooks.com

For our complete selection of fine books on this and related subjects,
please visit our website at *www.schifferbooks.com*. You may also write
for a free catalog.

Schiffer Publishing's titles are available at special discounts for
bulk purchases for sales promotions or premiums. Special editions,
including personalized covers, corporate imprints, and excerpts,
can be created in large quantities for special needs. For more
information, contact the publisher.

We are always looking for people to write books on new and
related subjects. If you have an idea for a book, please contact us at
proposals@schifferbooks.com.

CONTENTS

INTRODUCTION

Welcome to leatherworking. My approach to this craft will be for those who want a clearly traditional focus, who believe high quality matters, and who want to learn traditional techniques to use in modern ways. I hope you have many happy hours of enjoyment with this book and find it a useful companion on your leatherworking journey.

I have written my book as I would have liked to have been taught when I started working leather back in the late 1980s. I have broken each stage into easy-to-follow steps and built up the complexity of the projects as the book progresses. As you work through the projects, your confidence and command of the techniques will grow.

By no means are the techniques I cover in this book the only way to do the job—they are, however, all time-proven and work well.

Before you dive into the projects, take some time to familiarize yourself with the first section's chapters on the tools, skills, and techniques. Practice these until you have a good understanding of what you are doing and how to do it.

The projects are great fun, but the real value is in the skills you learn in the process. There is much enjoyment to be found in following the instructions for each project and making the items, but if I can encourage you to get down to the bones of a skill or technique, then the items you make can become your own designs, and you begin to really stand on your own two (leathercrafted) feet.

I have not necessarily chosen the most exciting projects—however, I have chosen those with high learning values. The skills required for each of these projects are all at the very core of leatherwork. Learn these and the exciting projects become achievable.

All that being said, learning from a book is not always easy. While I touch on the skills needed and give short explanations, every detail of every technique is just not possible to include in a book of this size.

If you find you are struggling with a particular technique, take a look at my online tutorials on the Armitage Leather channel on Vimeo. This is an online resource of videos to help tutor you in a great many techniques that you will find really useful. There are plenty of videos of the specific techniques I've used in this book, which may be clearer to follow.

If you wish to take leathercraft even further, book a face-to-face lesson here in the workshop or attend one of the many group courses offered.

View *www.armitageleather.com* for lots more information.

The measurements used in this book are in metric, which is a clear unit and will help you with precision. If you are able to work in metric, it will make things easier.
However, if you are more used to working with imperial measurements, these two charts can assist you with any conversions you may need.

mm	Inches
1	0.039
2	0.079
3	0.118
4	0.158
5	0.197
6	0.236
7	0.276
8	0.315
9	0.354
10	0.394
11	0.433
12	0.472
13	0.512
14	0.551
15	0.591
16	0.630
17	0.669
18	0.709
19	0.748
20	0.787
30	1.181
40	1.575
50	1.969
60	2.362
70	2.756
80	3.150
90	3.543
100	3.937

mm	Oz.
0.4	1
0.8	2
1.2	3
1.6	4
2	5
2.4	6
2.8	7
3.2	8
3.6	9
4	10
4.4	11
4.8	12

TOOLS AND TECHNIQUES

TOOL SELECTION

Choosing and using the right tool for the job is an important part of leathercraft, because it can make all the difference between success and failure. The temptation is to buy as many tools as cheaply as possible, in the belief that you can do more if you have more, but it is better to start out with fewer high-quality tools and work more effectively.

When starting out, you may struggle with a particular technique, and it will not always be clear if this is because you just need practice, or if the tool is working against you. At the outset, knowing that you are only working against your own limitations and that you have a tool you can trust is a good mental foundation with which to proceed. If you are second-guessing why something is going wrong and suspecting the tool, you are fighting two battles at once.

Always buy the best you can afford; if you pay for top quality, you cry only once!

The following is a list of some recommended tools to get you started. It is by no means a definitive list, but it will get you up and running. It's roughly in the order that you'll use them.

As the projects increase in complexity toward the end of the book, more tools will be needed. You do not, however, have to tackle everything at once. Take your time and build your skill set and toolbox slowly, and your development will become organic.

1. Saddler's clam: This is a very important piece of equipment designed to hold an item rock steady to allow you to saddle-stitch.

2. Irons: This tool is designed to mark the holes where you want to stitch. Traditionally these would be pricking irons, and then an awl would be used to make individual holes for each stitch. This takes a lot of time, practice, and skill. So instead, for beginners, I recommend using one of the new

stitching irons. These fully make the holes, allowing you to stitch without spending many long hours learning how to use an awl. You will need an awl at a later stage, but let's get you started first before tackling one.

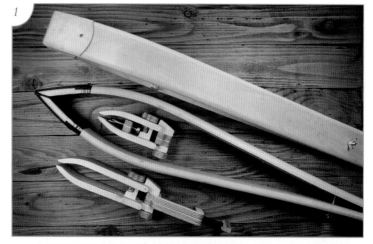

3. Pulling block: With the new irons acting like a row of awl blades, we need to ensure the iron comes out perfectly straight, the same as it went in. To help with this, use a small wooden block to keep the leather flat while pulling the iron out.

4. Knives: There are just too many to recommend one over the others, so instead I'll list the qualities you need to look for in a knife:

• Good steel—you will spend less time keeping it sharp.
• Thin, but not flexible—you don't want the blade to move under pressure.
• Comfort—a good, comfortable handle is essential.

5. Hammer/maul: This will mainly be used to strike irons and punches, but note that these tools are made of steel, so the hammer can't be. Steel on steel will damage your tools. Nylon or polymer is recommended; wood is too slick and can be damaged, and rubber will bounce. You are looking for a hammer or maul that will give a dead blow with no bounce that can cause a second strike—it's very frustrating if the tool moves between strikes and damages the leather.

6. Hole punch: Available as single and rotary options. This is the ideal tool to make round holes for belts, rivets, studs, and the like.

7. Rule: A steel rule is an invaluable tool for measuring and cutting against. Precision is important, so get a good one. A few different lengths will be helpful.

8. Cutting edge: This is a much-heavier tool than a rule. Rarely marked with any measurements, it is purely a guide for cutting. Thick and heavy and 2 inches wide is best.

9. Scratch awl: Also called a clickers awl. This small tool is basically a fine spike in a handle. It is the perfect tool for marking and drawing on leather.

10. Dividers: Also called wing dividers or a scratch compass, it is the perfect tool for tracing a fine line along the edge of leather that dictates the distance from the edge of the leather your stitching needs to be.

5

8

6

9

7

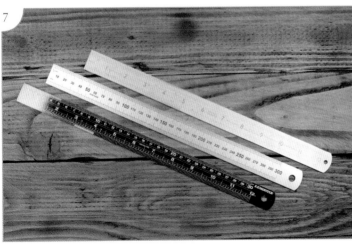

10

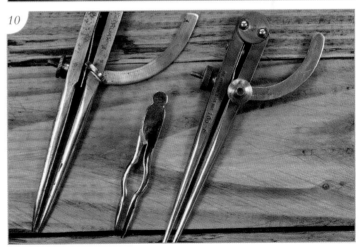

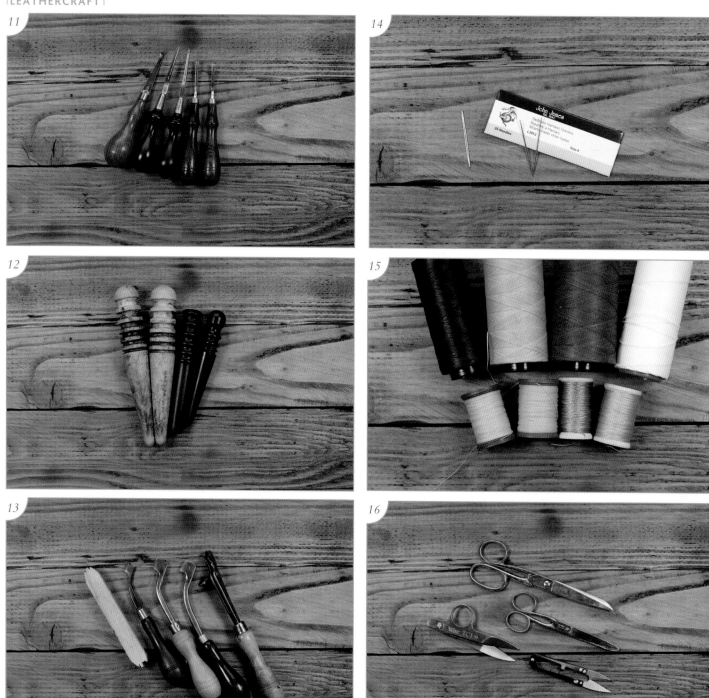

11

12

13

14

15

16

11. Edger: Also known as a beveler. This little tool is designed to take a fine bevel off the leather at the edge. It is the perfect tool to help dress edges and protect them from damage.

12. Slicker: A lovely little tool that when used with moisture or an edge compound slicks the edges of the leather down to a fine sheen.

13. Crease: This tool has two jobs: it adds a level of detail to plain leather edges and also prevents moisture from seeping in from the edge, preventing water stains.

14. Needles: Saddler's harness needles with blunt points are designed for stitching leather and are available in different sizes according to their use.

15. Thread: There are many variants of thread suitable for stitching leather, including linen, nylon, and polyester.

16. Snips/scissors: A must for snipping thread, since this needs to be done with a level of accuracy.

17. Cutting mat: While there are many boards available, a self-healing cutting mat is great, inexpensive, and widely available.

18. Crew punch: This is also called a bag or oblong punch. It is for adding the slit to a strip of leather where a buckle is going to sit, to allow the prong to pass through.

19. Strap punch: The perfect tool to put an English or round point on a strap for belts, bags, and watch straps.

20

21

22

23

24

25

20. Skiving knife: A very thin and sharp-angled knife for taking thin layers of leather off to thin strap ends or edges.

21. Corner cutters: If you are able to add corner cutters to your toolbox, you will find corners no longer difficult to cut. In the meantime, a good set of disks and a bit of patience will do the job.

22. Edge dressing: There are many products on the market today. Edge Kote and beeswax will get you started until you have had a chance to try the others.

23. Square: Any good-quality square that will give you an accurate right angle will do the job.

24. Setting hammer: A good dome-headed hammer or smasher will flatten your stitching or assist with the bonding of a glued edge.

25. Awls: While any stitching we undertake in the beginning is not reliant on an awl, there is very much still a place for one, especially a soft awl for multiple layers.

26. Strap cutter: An invaluable tool for cutting straps and even strips of leather.

27. Sanding tools: Any sandpaper will work for roughing up or sanding edges, but there are a few inexpensive tools that will help with these tasks; namely, sanding blocks and sanding sticks. These are not specific to leatherwork and are widely available at most hardware stores or online.

28. Bone folder: Traditionally a tool fashioned from the shin bone of a cow, it is designed to assist with the folding of leather, most commonly used by bookbinders. It is an ideal tool for creasing leather where a spine or fold is required or when the leather needs pushing in to the corners of a shape to create a raised area. The tool can be made of bone, horn, wood, or plastic.

MATERIALS AND HARDWARE

Unless you are based in the UK and have access to the same suppliers I use, it will be difficult to use the same materials and hardware I refer to and use for these projects. I have listed them at the back of the book should you be able to do so, but it's better to describe the type of leather used rather than being specific.

The majority of items in this book have been made using a "case" leather that is dyed-through vegetable-tanned shoulder. It is firm to the touch but still supple to use. This leather is easy to cut, marks well, and takes a good crease. It is also easy to finish the edges and bring to a nice shine. For the rest, bridle butt has been used.

I have included very little hardware, which will keep your costs down and the complexity to a sensible level. For each project I have listed the leather and hardware needed, but this is only a guideline, and different weights can be used if you wish. Do not be too enthusiastic about using thin leathers too early—they can be hard to manage if you are only just getting to grips with your techniques.

If you are intending to use tooling leather, see page 54 for more information about staining leather. The thickness or weight needed will remain the same.

Hardware is very much a personal choice. I use solid brass where I can in these projects, since it's long lived and extremely reliable. The rivets however are copper.

Project 1	Finger protectors	Pig skin, 2–3 oz. (1 mm)	
Project 2	Slip pouch	Case shoulder, 3–4 oz. (1.5 mm)	
Project 3	Pocket protector	Case shoulder, 3–4 oz. (1.5 mm)	14 g saddler's rivets
Project 4	Card holder	Case shoulder, 3–4 oz. (1.5 mm)	
Project 5	Pencil roll	Case shoulder, 3–4 oz. (1.5 mm)	
Project 6	Stitching-iron pouch	Case shoulder, 6–7 oz. (2.5 mm)	
Project 7	Passport cover	Case shoulder, 3–4 oz. (1.5 mm)	
Project 8	Belt	Bridle butt, 8–9 oz. (3.5 mm)	brass buckle, 1½ in.
Project 9	Gussetless bag	Case shoulder, 7–8 oz. (3 mm)	Sam Browne stud
Project 10	Knife sheath	Bridle shoulder, 7–8 oz. (3 mm)	
Project 11	Dice cup	Case shoulder, 8–9 oz. (3.5 mm)	
Project 12	Round-bottom bag	Case shoulder, 6–7 oz. (2.5 mm)	

At the back of the book is a list where you will find many of the suppliers of leather, hardware, and tools that I use, and a brief explanation of what can be found there.

MEASURING

Possibly one of the more critical skills in leatherwork. We are, after all, working toward getting several pieces of leather to fit together exactly so that they can be stitched. The better they are measured, the better the cut—the better the cut, the better the fit—and the better the result.

This is a foundational skill and sometimes not viewed with the importance it deserves. Preparation is the key along with having the right tools for the job.

A ridged metal rule is better than a cloth tape or retractable tape measure. It will also help to have several at different lengths.

Repeating measurements is one way of introducing unwanted variation. When working off a common edge, try to limit where you are measuring from. One way of doing this—and a good way to eliminate error— is to use a rule stop set at the desired measurement.

It's easy to fall into the trap that leather is forgiving and to adopt the mentality of "It'll be ok." It possibly will be, but the more effort that's put into measuring accurately, the less work we have to do putting it right at the other end.

Do not be too eager to get the leather cut: measure, measure again, test, and then cut.

Record your measurements clearly and in a consistent way. Generally, the first aspect we should measure is the width; therefore this is the first measurement we record. For example, let's say the width is 140mm and the height is 220mm, this should be recorded as 140 x 220mm, making the orientation portrait. If you recorded this as 200 x 140mm, this would make the piece landscape.

If it were just a rectangle, it's unlikely to be critical. But if you're fitting things together, your recording could make a catastrophic difference if it is the wrong way round.

A good rule to follow is "along the corridor and up the stairs." You cannot climb the stairs until you have gone along the corridor. By this rationale, the first measurement taken and recorded is always the width, then the height. Be consistent; it helps enormously.

Use a square when it's required to ensure a right angle, and always keep the rule flat.

The more care taken in measuring, the more accurate you will be in the construction and the better the result.

PATTERNMAKING

This process is absolutely essential and can form up to 60 percent of the time a completed project takes from concept to product.

You cannot cut or mark a piece of leather if you do not know where to cut and mark it.

Making a pattern or template is the perfect way to test your measurements and give you a visual representation of the item you are making. I cannot stress the value of a pattern or template strongly enough.

The projects in this book are relatively simple, but each will require a pattern, and where necessary this will be covered in the project. However, here are a few simple points on how to begin by creating a center line and how to achieve square cuts.

1. As an example, in the Slip Pouch project on page 64, a stiff card is used to make a template, measuring 111 x 156 mm.

We are going to make this template in paper here to show the process you will follow to build up more complex designs.

2. Use a stiff paper to create the pattern. Find a piece a little larger than that needed, in this case 111 x 156 mm.

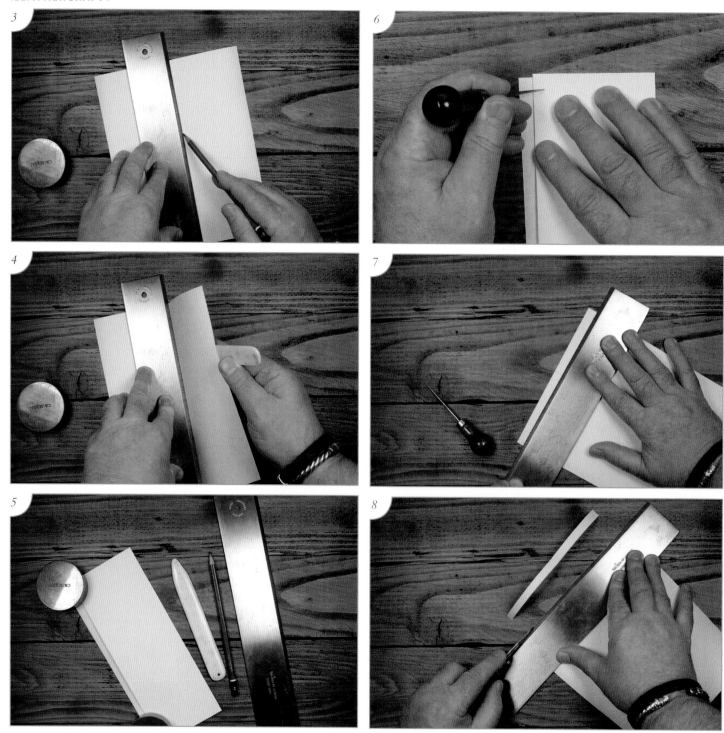

3. The first task is to create a center line. Roughly mark the center of a piece of paper bigger than 111 x 156 mm.

4. Place the rule over these marks and keep it in place until you have completed all these steps: Draw a line along the edge of the rule. Next, take a bone folder or something firm and slim, but not sharp. Run the bone folder under the paper against the rule, causing it to crease neatly up against the ruler.

5. This will make the paper fold in a perfectly straight line, and in this way make the center line.

6. The next step is to create a right angle at one end for us to measure from. Make a small hole through both sides at the open side of the fold at one end. When opened out, this will give you two small holes on either side of the paper.

7. These holes when lined up are at a perfect right angle to the center line.

8. You can now cut along the line between the two holes, making a right angle cut at one end.

9. If it is not clear which end is the right angle, mark the other with an X, so you don't measure from the wrong end. Now fold the paper. From the spine, we want to measure half the width needed: in this case we need 111 mm for our width, so set your rule stop to 5.5 mm, set this against the spine or fold, and mark three times lightly in pencil.

10. You can now cut along this line with the paper on the fold. If you have varied the measurement with the pencil, rule, or knife, the variation will be repeated on both sides. This will ensure the center line is still in the center. Open the paper, and it should be 111 mm wide.

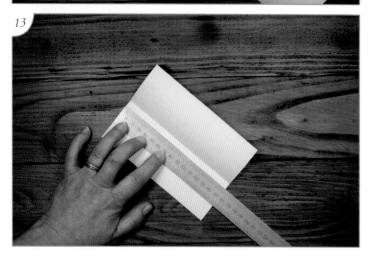

11. Close it again, and now from the right angle end, at the open side, make a small hole at 6 in. (156 mm) through both pieces. Open the paper and cut in a straight line between these two holes.

12. This will have set the height to 6 in. (156 mm) and also be a perfect right angle.

13. This technique is ideal for marking out where hardware, pockets, or holes need to be added, and keeps the piece symmetrical.

It is just a starting point for patternmaking. As you practice the projects and the patternmaking in each one, your skill set will grow and the template making will become second nature.

CUTTING LEATHER

Most of us have been cutting since the first time our parents let us use a knife. But when was the last time you really analyzed how you cut and why?

Leather is a unique material to cut—different thicknesses will cut differently, and shoulder will cut differently to butt. It is hard to find one way to cover all the options.

Whatever the leather or thickness, many common issues concern such things as sliding rules, stringy cuts, little tabs sticking out at the end of cuts, and the material moving. Believe it or not, we tend to cause most of these problems ourselves.

To help resolve these issues, let's look at a few areas that will help us improve—**preparation**, **angle**, **power**, and **accuracy**.

1.   Preparation. A cluttered bench will cause you to compromise your technique because you will be trying to work around obstacles and through mess. Take the time to tidy up and get your preparation in order.

2.   If your patternmaking is good, you will have assembled a parts list. This means you'll be doing all of your cutting first. It's like any technique: if you prepare and approach it properly, it will go well.

Angle. In terms of cutting angle, people are bifocal, and we like to have what we are about to cut visually straight, either horizontally or vertically, so we either cut across or toward us. It's a visual thing.

This looks to be a good cut at the outset.

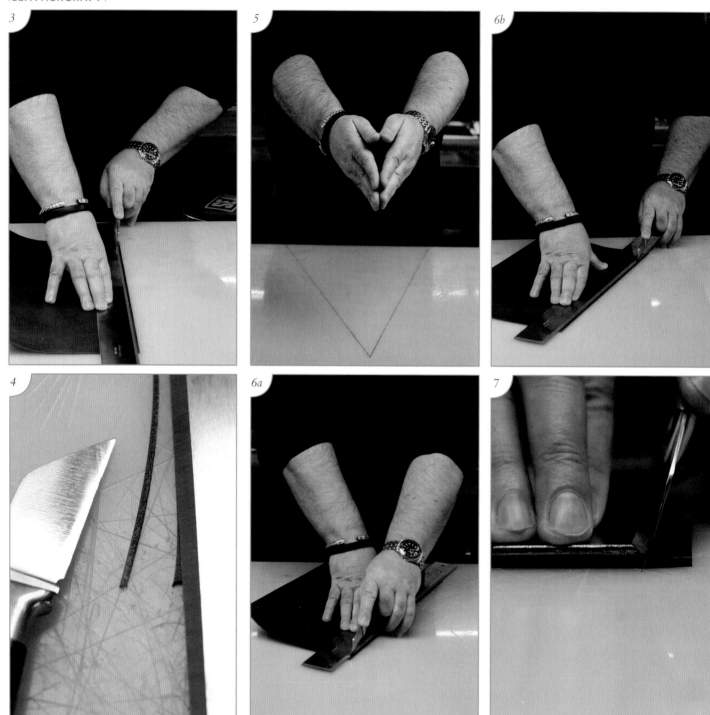

3. However, we can see here how much the elbow has had to move out as the arm reaches the body—changing the angle of the wrist and in turn the angle of the knife.

4. It is this posture that causes that little tail at the end of the cut to appear.

5. We must keep the blade straight throughout the whole cut, and the best way to do this is to keep our knife, hand, and forearm as straight as possible. This means cutting at the correct angle. Stand at the board with your arms outstretched and palms together. Imagine a dot on the board where your fingers meet, and a further dot at each shoulder.

Draw a line between these dots, creating a triangle. Cutting inside this triangle is less than ideal; cutting just outside this line will give you a far better cut since it allows the elbow to pass the body, keeping the knife, hand, and arm straight. This achieves a far greater level of accuracy and cutting consistency.

6. This approach will give you a far better angle for cutting. Here we can see a good, clear space between the body and cutting arm.

7. At the end of the cut, there is still a gap between the cutting arm and the body, while the forearm, hand, and knife are still in a straight line.

Power. Too much is bad. Too often we approach a cut with the mindset of "I will cut this leather in one try," applying a lot of power to the cutting hand. What may not be clear is that the more power we apply to our cutting hand, the more power we also apply to the hand holding the rule. The rule hand compensates for balance. So . . . rather than rule slipping, which is what we think we are stopping it from doing, we are, in fact, pushing it.

Accuracy. Do not try at the outset to cut through the leather in one try. Be gentle with the knife, hold it loosely at the end of the handle, and draw it across the leather; accuracy is key. It may not feel like you have cut the leather, but you have. You have created a very fine channel that will help guide the blade on the second pass.

It is far better to cut three or four times to get an accurate cut, than to cut it in one go and get it wrong. A rough edge is easier to deal with than a misshapen piece.

The last thing to consider is undercutting. This happens when the knife is held at a slight angle and the tip of the blade is not in line with the edge of the rule. In fact it actually goes under the rule. This will cut the leather at an angle—an undercut. On a single piece, this can be lost in edging (beveling) and slicking, but on multiple pieces, some drastic sanding may be required that completely changes the shape of your piece.

8. The simple tactic to avoid that: keep the blade vertical when cutting.

CUTTING CORNERS

1. Without doubt, one of the best ways of cutting a corner is with a corner-cutting tool. However, you may not have one of these, or if you do it may not be the right size for the job at hand. So, we need to look for alternatives, and one of the best ways is to have a selection of disks, washers, and coins to cut around.

Once we have found the right size of disk, we need to choose the best way to cut around it. The temptation is to follow the curve and try to cut it in one sweep. On larger curves this will work, but on smaller, tighter curves, it will not.

This diagram of a right angle has marks made 5 mm apart and numbered 1 to 15 from top to bottom, and 1 to 15 from left to right.

You can see that a line has been drawn between each corresponding number: 1–1, 2–2, and so on. The result is that where each line meets, a curve appears because of the slight change in angle of each line.

Now imagine each line as a cut. Instead of cutting around the disk in one curved line, cut around it in fifteen straight lines.

2. This is a lengthier process and will take practice, but it gives a far more accurate and repeatable result to your corners. However, if you are able to get the right tool for the job, it will make life easier, especially on the tighter corners.

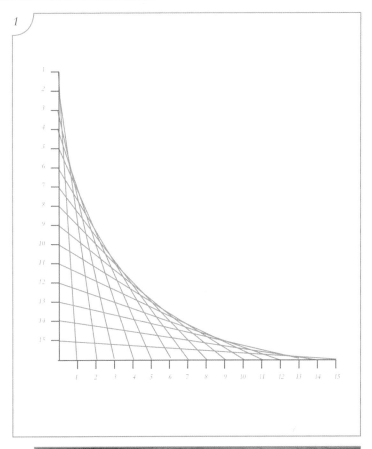

STITCHING

1. There are many and various ways to stitch leather, or more specifically, to make the holes through which to stitch.

The stitch we will be focusing on is known as English saddle stitch. This is where two needles (one in each hand) work on the same single, centered thread to produce two running stitches along the seam at the same time. This is done in such a way that the stitches sit at a slight but consistent angle, giving a pleasing look to the stitch and adding a high level of detail.

2. Traditionally, a pricking wheel or pricking iron is used to mark the stitching out, then an awl is used to actually make the holes, and then the stitching can be completed with thread.

The pricking iron only just penetrates the surface of the leather enough to clearly mark the location of the holes.

The pricking iron or wheel is the simple part of this process, and in this style of stitching, all the skill lies in the use of the awl.

Stitching position is the first key to ensuring you place the awl into the leather in a consistent way. The awl then has to be pushed into the hole with the angle of the blade matched to the angle of the hole, with the blade being perpendicular to the leather on both the horizontal and vertical planes.

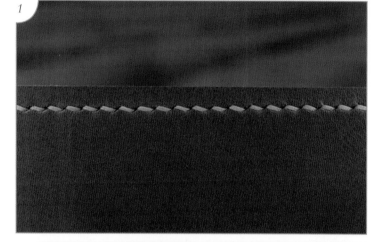

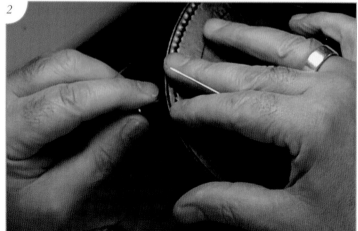

3. The depth at which the awl is pushed into the leather also has to be consistent, since varying this changes the hole size, thereby in turn changing the stitch length.

This technique, while being traditional and pleasing, takes some time to master, and trying to accrue the correct skills to do so would take you the best part of this book. In view of this, a modern style of tool will be employed; namely, the stitching iron.

Almost identical to the untrained eye, the stitching iron has longer and slimmer teeth and is capable of fully penetrating the leather in one strike. These more modern tools are composed of a much-higher grade of metal, which makes this possible.

4. Being able to strike and iron all the way through a piece of leather is like having twelve awl blades in a row—this offers a greater level of stitching consistency for people new to leatherwork.

More importantly, the stitching on the back of items can now be of a higher standard. This is important since small leather goods are usually seen and handled from all angles, and the back of our stitching must be able to bear close scrutiny.

Getting consistent stitching on the back of an item with an awl was one of the steeper learning curves of traditional saddle stitch.

5. The first order of business in getting a good row of stitching is to have a good stitch line. This is the line you will follow with your irons and is made using a short set of dividers, which have a polished spike on each side.

6. Once you have created your stitch line, the irons are placed onto that line and struck until they have penetrated the leather to the desired depth. It helps if you place the leather onto a small pad or piece of thick leather to cushion the blow, since this allows the iron to go a little deeper through the leather by letting the teeth poke out of the back.

7. Now we have a row of holes that we can stitch directly without the need of an awl. This is certainly the case for simple seams, although more complex seams may still require the use of an awl. Very much like an awl, the iron needs to go in straight; if it is struck at an angle, the stitch line on the back will not be right.

8. The iron also needs to come out as it went in—straight. For this we use a small block of wood called a pulling block to hold the leather fast while the iron is pulled out. Pulling the iron out at an angle will damage the holes or even, over time, damage the teeth of the tool.

9. Once the holes have been made, we are ready to stitch. Get enough thread—eight times the length of the seam is more than enough. It is better to have too much than not enough, so don't be stingy with your thread.

Thread a needle onto each end, piercing the tail of the thread with the needle to leave a small loop.

10. Now we are ready to stitch. There are many ways to do this, but if you struggle, check out my Vimeo channel, where I go into a lot of detail.

A good clam to hold the item steady, and we are ready. I am going to describe this for a right-handed person. If you are left-handed, replace the word "*right*" with "*left*," and it still works.

Place the leather into the clam, with the face side facing right. You will be stitching toward yourself, so place the leather in the clam with the farthest hole at the far side of the clam.

Start with two backstitches. I am using braided polyester thread, which can be heated when cut to prevent the thread from going back through the hole. I end with two backstitches.

11. This is raised a little higher than it should be, but I have done this to make the explanation clearer. You want the holes as close to the top on the clam as you can get them while still being able to stitch comfortably.

Place the first needle (your right-hand needle) into the third hole from the end, and center your thread.

Backstitching

1. Begin stitching: the first two stitches are away from us; place the right-hand needle halfway into the second hole from the end.

On the back of the leather you'll see a thread and a needle sticking out.

2. Place the second needle (*left*) between the thread and needle in the gap.

3. Whichever hand you use, and whether stitching toward or away from you, if you follow this process the thread will always be in the right position, and your stitch will look good.
With your finger and thumb, create a cross with the two needles, with the left needle pointing up.

4. Do not let go of this until the second needle is back in the hole. Holding the cross, draw the thread through the hole to the left. Now turn the cross so the left needle is pointing toward the back of the leather.

5. Place this needle into the hole being stitched, ensuring that it goes at the back of the thread, so the needle is still in the gap between the two threads.

As you look at this from above, you'll see thread, needle, thread.

6. On the right side of the leather, gently pull the thread that is in the hole with the needle; this is to find out if you have pierced the thread with the needle. If you have, pull the thread in line with the needle until it slides off the end. There is no need to take the needle out of the hole. Draw all the thread through the hole until the loops disappear.

7. We now need to look at the tension and how much to apply. Every leather is different, and the tension you apply to one will not be right for another. We will therefore make this a visual thing: if you look down at the piece you are stitching, you will see both sides of the stitch you have just made.

8. Hold the thread securely so it does not slip through your hands, then pull gently but firmly until you see both sides of the stitch seat snugly into the leather.

7

8

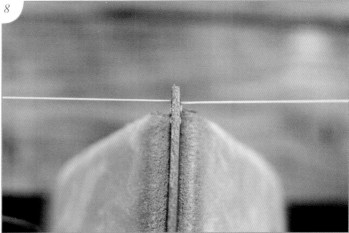

9. As soon as you see it disappear from sight, stop. When you let go the stitch will reappear, but that is as it should be.

In fact, the concern is pulling too strongly and ripping the leather between the holes, so take care to stop the moment you see the threads settle in.

That is the first backstitch completed, and you are now ready to repeat this process for the second. Go back and reread this section to repeat for the second stitch.

9

Stitching toward You

Once you have stitched your two backstitches into place, you are now ready to begin stitching toward you.

The process is very similar, with one small addition: the cast.

1. To begin, place the right-hand needle halfway into the next hole to stitch. Again, we will see on the left-hand side a needle and a thread; place the second needle in the gap between the needle and thread and complete the stitch as before.

We are now stitching holes that have already been stitched, so this may be a little tougher.

Rubbing your needles lightly with beeswax will give you a better grip on them.

We also need to lay the stitches so they look nice; there is already a stitch in place here, and we don't want the thread looking bulky or messy. What we can do to avoid this is to sit one stitch next to the other.

Before closing the stitch, take one of the needles and, making sure the loop is above the needle, place it on top of the existing stitch.

2. Keeping the needle in place, apply tension to the thread on the left; this will cause the thread to ride up the needle like a ramp guiding it to sit next to the existing thread.

3. Once done, remove the needle and have a look; you will see both stitches sitting neatly side by side. This prevents one stitch sitting high over the other and therefore exposed to being rubbed and worn.

4. Moving on to the cast—this is relevant only if you are stitching right-handed with standard irons. If you are stitching left-handed, using reverse irons or backstitching, you don't need to cast.

The cast makes the stitching look better. It encourages the threads to twist in such a way that it causes the angle of the stitch to be a little stronger. The idea is that threads pass in such a way in the hole that they twist.

Once you have put the second needle in the hole you're currently stitching, you will see the following: thread, needle, thread, with one hole containing both a needle and a thread.

5. It is this thread in the hole with the needle that you take; lift it up over the needle and away from you. This is the cast, ensuring the threads pass the right way to angle the stitch.

6. If you forget to cast, the stitch will not sit correctly and will look flat—check out the photo. If you can't see it, it's the fifth and sixth stitches sitting incorrectly.

When complete, draw out all the slack, hold the thread firmly, and apply sufficient tension to seat the thread.

Repeat this process for every stitch. Never try to rush this stage; with practice, you will begin to stitch efficiently. Do not try to do it quickly—take your time.

The old saying "More haste, less speed" definitely applies here!

One final thing to mention on stitching is the impact it can have on internal measurements. On many items this will not matter, but where we are making a small item for contents that are quite specific, such as card holders, notebook covers, wallets, and the like, it becomes rather important.

The stitch line is just the line we add to follow with our irons; our stitching, however, does not sit within the width of this line. It sits much wider; depending on the iron, each stitch hole is at least 2 mm long and sits at an angle.

This means our actual stitching can be up to 2 mm wider than our line; in view of this we will add a +1 mm to our stitch line when it has an impact on an internal measurement.

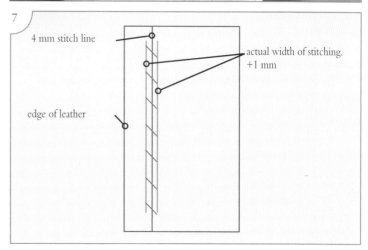

4 mm stitch line

actual width of stitching.
+1 mm

edge of leather

EDGE DRESSING

Edge dressing is an ideal way to professionally finish the edges of leather, by taking the quality of the object up to the next level.

The leather used in these projects is vegetable tanned, so we are going to be looking at how to dress edges to suit that leather. This will include creasing, edging, slicking, and applying Edge Kote (or similar coating product).

Creasing

1. Creasing leather has a twofold purpose. First, it finishes off the edge of a plain piece of leather that would otherwise have no adornment, by adding a nice level of detail. Second, and more importantly, it compresses the fibers of the leather at the edge and so prevents moisture wicking into the leather and causing water stains.

2. Depending on the leather, it can be applied both hot and cold.

Vegetable-tanned leather (or veg-tan) can be creased cold with wood or metal.

Wood will burnish a crease into the leather and gives a lovely darkened line.

3. A cold metal crease will add a nice detailed line but will not burnish, and in time this can push out. In this image a purse crease is being used.

4. Another version is the screw crease, this is the same as the purse crease. Both can be heated, which will iron a sharp line into the leather and be more permanent.

Other leather such as bridle and chrome can be creased only by using a hot iron.

Another benefit of hot creasing is that less pressure is needed to apply a line, so more accuracy can be achieved. However, this is a skill that needs a lot of practice, especially on curves and corners.

Edging/Beveling

The idea behind this technique is to remove sharp corners from the leather that can otherwise be knocked, caught, and damaged. Edging/beveling leather has much the same principle as used in woodwork.

This tool is used to cut a small strip of leather from the bottom and top edges of the leather in order to leave a fine slanting edge or bevel, making the end softer to the touch and less prone to damage. In English this tool is named for its result, a beveler.

1. If a fine edger is used, a fine edge is made. This is ideal for thin leather or if a flat edge is required on thicker leather.

2. Using a larger edger will take off more leather and leave more prominently rounded edges. Such a rounded edge is very desirable on tactile items such as handles, reins, bag straps, and belts.

3. The photo shows the removed strips of leather side by side and gives an indication on how little or how much leather can be removed with the different tools.

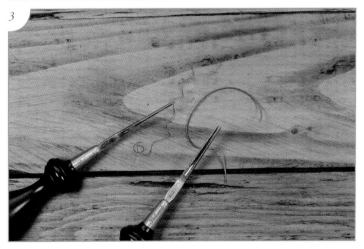

4

5

6

7

8

Slicking

4. Once you have used the edger, the leather fibers at the edge will be rough to the touch; these will need bedding in. Wooden slickers, such as those pictured, help do the job.

5. Applying a bespoke solution to the leather edges will soften the fibers and make them more malleable and soft enough to slick down. You can use water, gum tragacanth (a natural gum), or *tokonole* (a Japanese natural wax).

Once a light solution has been applied, the edge can be slicked by applying an even pressure and rubbing in line with the edge of the leather.

6. Too much pressure and the leather will crush; too much rubbing and the edge can dry out and begin to rough up again.

This is an image of the edge of the leather; we can see that the edger used was large enough to round the edge, and the slicker has finished off the job to give a pleasing round edge to the leather.

7. A good slicker will have a groove that will match the edge you are trying to achieve. Use this to rub the edge to round it off. However, slicking needs to be done for only as long as it takes for the edge to feel smooth. If you overslick an edge too much, the leather will become too smooth and products such as Edge Kote will not stick and, if they do, will peel off later.

8. Once a clean and smooth edge has been achieved, lightly sand it to create a key for the Edge Kote (or similar) to adhere to. It may seem counterproductive to smooth an edge off just to rough it up again, but having a consistent edge is important, and making it porous is vital for any product to be able to adhere to it.

Staining

Adding a stain or paint to the edge of leather not only adds a fine level of detail but also protects the leather edge against the elements working with the crease. Once you have chosen your desired product, it is vital that you test it on a small piece of leather. Note that some dyes not designed for edge work will bleed into the leather; if you are using a contrasting color, this could spoil the item. For this demonstration I used Edge Kote, since its viscosity is greater than dye, so it will not penetrate as deeply and stain the leather.

1. Once a piece of leather has been edged, lightly slicked, and sanded, it is ready for the surface coating. This is applied in three stages. First the spine; this is the largest area, so more product is needed, and I found that a pencil is an ideal applicator for this slightly tricky bit.

2. At the same time as you apply the coating, you can use the pencil as a slicker, bedding the solution into the fibers. Once the spine is covered, apply less product to the pencil and begin to follow the bevel edge lines.

3. The cleaner the bevel line, the cleaner this edge will look. Start with the inside to get the feel of the angle and amount of coating needed, and when you're happy, apply to the outside. Let it dry thoroughly—don't rush this part. If the edge is uneven and rough (which can happen), sand lightly and reapply.

This is very much like sanding wood between coats of varnish; as you apply moisture, the grain will lift and need sanding back. Once you're happy with your finish, rub with beeswax and slick again.

4. This will apply heat to the beeswax, which will bond with the surface coating and bed in nicely.

5. A good rub with a cloth and you are done.

BEGINNER PROJECTS

FINGER PROTECTORS

You may have noticed from the style of the items in this book that I am a maker of robust items in a heavy leather that are stitched entirely by hand. Some of the heavier items, such as the belt, sheath, and pouches, will require a reasonable amount of tension when being stitched. This can be uncomfortable when using some threads—worse still, if not held firmly enough, the thread can slide and cut into your fingers when you apply firm tension. With time, calluses will build up, offering some protection, but until that happens, leathercrafters run the risk of sore fingers. So, leather sleeves are a very useful thing to have in your toolbox if you are going to sew by hand, to put over your fingers when you're stitching.

TOOLS & MATERIALS

Cloth tape measure	Pulling block
Rule	Maul or hammer
Dividers	Needles—no. 4
Knife	Thread—0.6 mm
Stitching or pricking irons—7 spi	Stitching clam
	Scissors or snips

Pigskin, 2–3 oz. (1 mm)

With the amount of stitching coming up in this book, together with the weight of leather we are going to use, finger protectors are the first project for you to make—so you have them ready for the other projects. Look after those fingers and they will look after you!

Even though I have built up calluses on my little fingers, when I am stitching heavy items in bridle leather I still use finger protectors.

1 The design is extremely simple: a piece of thin leather stitched into a tube, turned, and worn on the finger to apply tension to the thread when stitching.

I favor my little fingers, but others prefer the index finger. It all depends on how you grip your thread. I pinch it between my thumb and forefinger, grip it with my three remaining fingers, and pull with the thread resting against the outside of my little finger.

2 Everyone's hand is different, so there's no point in giving measurements. The important thing is to look at how to measure your fingers to get the right size.

My little fingers are about 70 mm in circumference, so this is my starting point. I want the seam on the inside and the edges of the leather to sit flat, so I'm going for a 5 mm stitch line. Once stitched, this will give me enough leather to flatten down. Also, note that 5 mm needs to be added to both sides of the leather. Add another 5 mm to this measurement to allow you to get the sleeve on and off comfortably— wiggle room, if you like.

This gives a total width of 85 mm. If you keep the 5 mm stitch line (x 2) and 5 mm wiggle room, the equation is quite easy: the circumference of your finger plus 15 mm.

My index finger is 80 mm in circumference, so I need a 95 mm piece of leather, and so it goes.

3 The height of the leather is the measurement from where the finger leaves the hand to the second knuckle— in my case 50mm.

When stitching, fingers are rarely held straight, so keeping the sleeves in place isn't an issue, and we don't need to add anything extra.

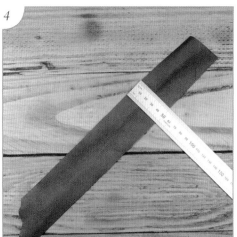

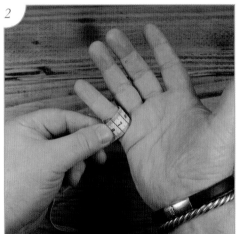

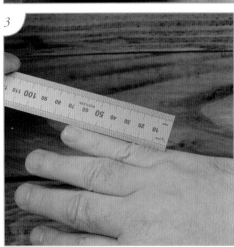

4 The leather we use is important. It must be strong but flexible enough so the finger can bend.

I am going to use a 2–3 oz. pigskin; a thin suede or deer skin will also do the job nicely.

So, measure your fingers and make your parts' list, in my case this is two 85 x 50 mm pigskin pieces.

This is one of the few items that you can tackle without a pattern or template. Cut a strip of leather 50 mm wide and, from this, cut two 85 mm lengths.

5 Once your pieces have been cut, mark your 5 mm stitch line on both sides of each piece.

6 Now to add the holes. Since the seam is to be turned, it will be pulled apart when stretched. Normal irons will create a slot, and the stitching will sit on one side when the seam is stretched, thus exposing the other side. To ensure this doesn't happen, use round irons and make round holes.

7 You can do this with normal irons if that's all you have, but if you are regularly going to work with items that require turned seams, round irons will be a good investment.

8 Once all the holes have been made, stitch the ends of the leather together to form a loop. Since I want to have the grain side of the leather on the outside, I fold the leather so the grain is on the inside while I stitch.

9 Once it's stitched, open the seam out and, with a dowel on the inside, tap the seam down. A little PVA glue will help keep the flaps in place.

10 Once that's done, turn the loop so the grain is outside and the sleeves are ready for use. Try them on: see how they fit.

It will take a bit of time to get them to mold to your shape and for you to get used to wearing them, but after a while they become an extension of your hand.

SLIP POUCH

This is an excellent project to begin your leatherwork journey. It is simple, requires minimal tools, takes only a few hours, and is inexpensive. By doing this piece you will gain a basic understanding of patternmaking, cutting, stitching, and dressing. The size can be adjusted to suit many different purposes, but in this instance I have chosen a notebook with the dimensions 89 mm wide, 140 mm high, and 4 mm thick.

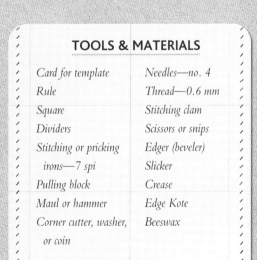

TOOLS & MATERIALS

Card for template	Needles—no. 4
Rule	Thread—0.6 mm
Square	Stitching clam
Dividers	Scissors or snips
Stitching or pricking irons—7 spi	Edger (beveler)
	Slicker
Pulling block	Crease
Maul or hammer	Edge Kote
Corner cutter, washer, or coin	Beeswax

Case shoulder, 3–4 oz. (1.5 mm)

1 The first task is to ensure the slip will fit the item for which it is intended. If you have not yet done so, now is a good time to familiarize yourself with the section on measuring (see pp. 22–23), since there are additional measurements that you also need.

Let's look first at the width of the slip, because we will be working from the center out. We know the item width is 89 mm. Next, we will be following a 4 mm stitch line—and we need to add 1 mm to allow for the actual width of the stitching, plus a bit of wiggle room to be able to get the item in and out. Forget the wiggle room, and the slip will be too tight. But 4 mm on either side will suffice for a single notebook.

2 The thickness of the item also has a part to play. In this case it's 4 mm, and we will add half the thickness to our formula on either side.

The result is a formula that lets us make slips for items of different sizes.

Since this slip will be used vertically (portrait), our figures look like this:

Stitch line	4 mm	Constant
Stitch width	1 mm	Constant
Wiggle room	4 mm	Constant
Half item thickness	*2 mm*	*Variable*
Item width	*89 mm*	*Variable*
Half item thickness	*2 mm*	*Variable*
Wiggle room	4 mm	Constant
Stitch width	1 mm	Constant
Stitch line	4 mm	Constant

This gives a figure of **111 mm** for the total width. Change the item thickness and width but keep the rest, and it all still works.

3 Now the height. The notebook is 140 mm high. For this formula, we will be working from the top down.

We will want the notebook to sit inside the slip a little—5 mm will be enough to protect it—so this is our first measurement. We'll call it the cover. Our second measurement is the notebook itself. Now add half the thickness of the notebook, the stitch width, and the stitch line, which makes our template look like this:

Cover	*5 mm*	*Variable*
Item height	*140 mm*	*Variable*
Half item thickness	*2 mm*	*Variable*
Wiggle room	4 mm	Constant
Stitch width	1 mm	Constant
Stitch line	4 mm	Constant

As you can see, this gives a figure of **156 mm** for the total height.

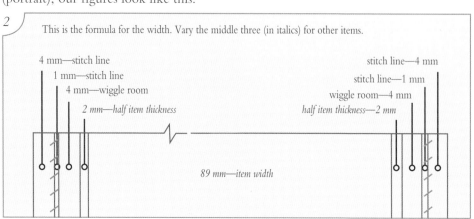

2 — This is the formula for the width. Vary the middle three (in italics) for other items.

4 mm—stitch line
1 mm—stitch line
4 mm—wiggle room
2 mm—half item thickness

stitch line—4 mm
stitch line—1 mm
wiggle room—4 mm
half item thickness—2 mm

89 mm—item width

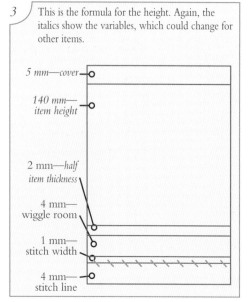

3 — This is the formula for the height. Again, the italics show the variables, which could change for other items.

5 mm—cover

140 mm—item height

2 mm—half item thickness

4 mm—wiggle room

1 mm—stitch width

4 mm—stitch line

4 For a slip of this kind, it is worth noting that there is a maximum thickness—about 10 mm—that we can fit inside before the corners begin to distort. If you go any thicker than 10 mm, you will probably need to think about adding a gusset.

Armed with all the information about the size of leather needed, it is time to make a template. You may think there is little need to do this when stitching two simple rectangles together, but this is not the case.

This slip will be stitched together using a single row of stitching, a simple seam. We need to ensure that the beginning stitch and the end stitch at the top of the slip are in line, and we need a template to achieve this.

Only one template is needed since it can be used for both pieces of leather.

Cut it from a stiff card, 111 mm wide x 156 mm high.

Round the corners; I have cut mine using a 21 mm corner cutter. Look at the chapter on corner cutting (see pp. 34–35) for information on how to do this.

5 Now draw a center line on your card, top to bottom, at 55.5 mm—half the width. Use dividers to mark a line 4 mm from the edge and around the outside of the card, starting on one side, down toward and around the first corner, across the bottom, round the second corner, and up the other side. This will be the stitch line—the line you

follow for marking your stitch holes.

When marking the stitch holes on the template, it is easy to vary the holes from one side to the other, especially at the corners. To stop this, add way lines—a set of lines that sit either side of the corners, making it easy to ensure the holes are symmetrical.

Add a way line to the top to indicate where the stitching will start and stop.

Using your rule stop, set to 10 mm, add a line 10 mm from the edge on all four sides of the card.

6 With all the lines needed marked out on the template, it is time to start adding the holes.

Make the first hole at the center point at the bottom of the card, where the center line crosses the stitch line.

Your iron has more than one tooth, but it doesn't matter which tooth you put on the cross. As long as one of the teeth of the iron is on this cross, that is your center hole.

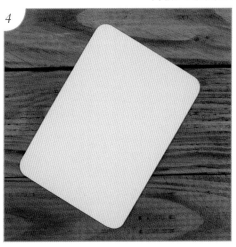

4

5

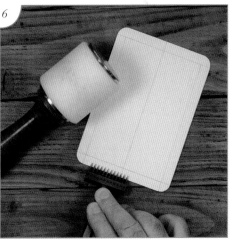

6

7 From this center hole, work out to the left, marking holes on your stitch line, stopping at the first way line.

Having done so, do the same to the right. You should see that the two holes at either end of this line are the same distance from the way lines on each side.

Now, mark your holes around the corner on the left, stopping at the second way line.

Do the same to the corner on the right, and you will see that the same number of holes appears between the way lines on both sides, with the last two holes being in the same position. If this is the case, continue marking the holes up both sides of the template, stopping just before the way line at the top.

If the last hole sits on the line, that's fine, but it should not go over the line. It's better to stop slightly short.

A quick count of holes to ensure you have the same on both sides will confirm your symmetry.

With practice, all the holes will line up; the top two will be parallel and there will be no long or short stitches.

This technique for prepricking features heavily in this book and is worth practice. It is a sure way to achieve high-quality stitching on both the front and the back and removes the guesswork from stitching round corners.

8 Now you are ready to cut the leather. Here I used 1.5 mm thick finished shoulder. Use a similar leather for similar results.

Cut two pieces to the same size as the template, 111 x 115 mm, and trim your corners neatly. If your corners are sharp or rough, you can soften them with a sanding block.

9 Overlay your template and gently mark through the end holes of each straight run and all holes on the corners. Make sure your irons are perfectly vertical for this, or the holes will come out in a different position on the leather.

10 Now that you can see where the top two holes are, run your dividers around where the holes will be made— 4 mm from the edge of the leather.

Following the marks and the stitch line, fully mark and make all your holes on both pieces of leather.

If any of the marks you made for the holes are not sitting on the line, follow the line rather than the marks. The marks should disappear when you make the holes properly, even if you are a little off.

7

8

9

11 Having fully marked and made all of your holes, you are now ready to dress the edges that are not going to be stitched together—for this project, this will be the tops of the leather where there are no stitch holes.

Depending on the tool you have, add a crease to the leather. If you do not have a crease, use the dividers to make a fine line.

Now, bevel, slick, and apply edge paint or coat to the edge, giving it a final slick with beeswax.

The edges along the stitching will be dressed as one piece once the leather has been stitched. The edge dressing section (see pp48–55) covers this process.

12 You are almost done. Using a good stable clam and following the techniques outlined in the section on stitching (see pp36–45), stitch the two pieces together.

Now it's time to dress the remaining edges. Doing this after stitching them together gives a far more even finish. Dressing these edges uses the same process at outlined in Step 11, except no crease is needed because the stitching is already there.

Once you have completed the stitching and dressing, the slip is finished. Use a bone folder to open out the seams on the inside of the slip and insert your notebook.

10

11

12

POCKET PROTECTOR

How many holes have been made in the pockets of pants and jeans by shoving sharp tools into them over the years? I know I have a terrible habit of putting screwdrivers and scissors into my back pocket when I'm working, and I've lost a few tools through the holes they made. A pocket protector is one of those things that you didn't know you needed until you've seen one. It's not just limited to pants; it is an ideal addition to a bib or apron, or just a good way of keeping your screwdrivers or scissors together.

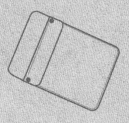

TOOLS & MATERIALS

Card for template	Rivet-setting tool—14 g
Rule	End cut pincers
Square	Needles—no. 4
Dividers	Thread—0.6 mm
Stitching or pricking	Stitching clam
irons—7 spi	Scissors or snips
Pulling block	Edger (beveler)
Maul or hammer	Slicker
Corner cutter, washer,	Crease
or coin	Edge Kote
2.5 mm hole punch	Beeswax
Saddler's rivets—14 g	

Case shoulder, 3–4 oz. (1.5 mm)

Building on what we have achieved so far, here the patternmaking is a little more complex. There is more stitching and dressing this time, and the design will have a pair of saddler's rivets. I am not normally a fan of rivets, but this design suits them well. There is a small issue where two lines of stitching need to meet but can't because of the design. A well-placed rivet resolves this and gives you an opportunity to use them and see how they are fitted.

1 First, we need a set of dimensions—in this instance, we are working to the internal dimensions of the back pocket of a pair of jeans. Measuring from the inside of the pocket, the illustrated example is 140 mm wide at the top, 130 mm wide at the bottom, and 140 mm deep. For now we will keep the item straight and work to the narrowest measurement.

At the start of your leathercrafting journey, function needs to take priority over form. Once you know something works, you can play with the design. For example, adding a taper to make it look nicer, but for now the goal is to get a working product.

2 We're going to need two further measurements: how deep the flap that sits over the outside of the pocket should be, and how high up we want the back to sit above the opening.

These are dimensions you can play with, but for now I will choose 30 mm for both.

Letting the dimensions dictate the design like this is the easiest way to get a working idea of how the item will look. This drawing identifies the dimensions of the pocket—internal and external—with dotted lines, and the protector with a solid line. The protector is 10 mm less than the internal pocket width, so it can go in and out of the pocket comfortably and will fit snugly at the bottom.

The length has not changed, because the addition of the rivets means it will sit higher in the pocket, since the bottom of the rivets will sit on the top of the pocket.

Note that both the 30 mm flap and the raised section have been added, and all the corners will be cut to a 20 mm diameter.

Using these measurements, the design has almost created itself.

Parts list

There are three parts to our pocket protector:

1. Back   120 x 170 mm
2. Front   120 x 140 mm
3. Flap   120 x 30 mm

3 Create three templates. Since the width of 120 mm is common to each part, an easy way to do this is to cut one piece of card to 120 mm and long enough to get all three pieces from it: 170 + 140 + 30 = 340 mm, but allow 400 mm to cover any errors.

One you have cut the card to 120 x 400 mm, add a center line before cutting each piece out. It's much easier than having to do it to each piece separately, and there will be a greater level of consistency.

4 On the long template, ensure you are starting with a right angle and begin to mark and cut your pieces. Start with the biggest piece: if you make a mistake, you can make a bigger piece into a smaller piece—the reverse is somewhat problematic.

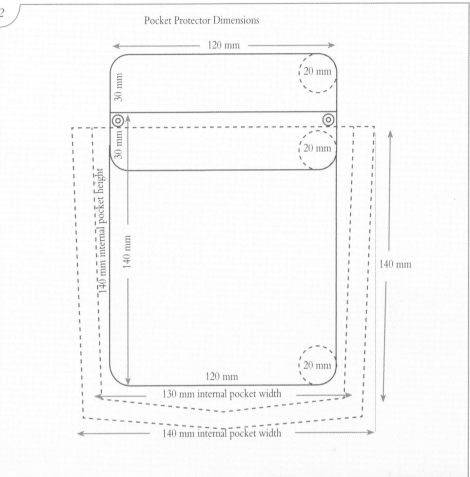

Pocket Protector Dimensions

120 mm

20 mm

30 mm

30 mm

20 mm

140 mm internal pocket height

140 mm

140 mm

20 mm

120 mm

130 mm internal pocket width

140 mm internal pocket width

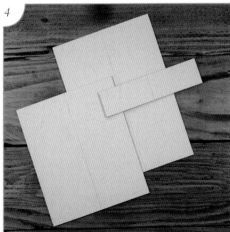

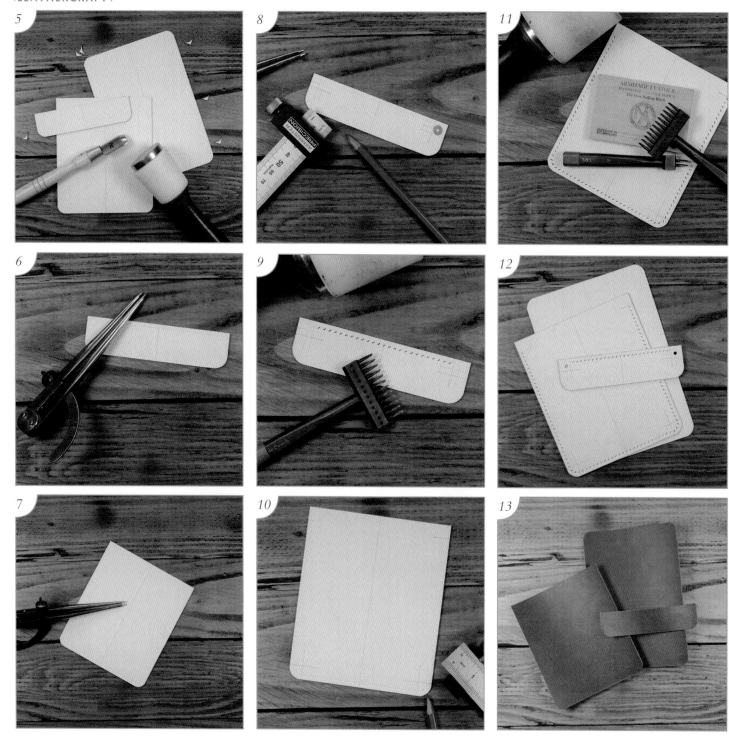

5 Round the corners now. I've used a 21 mm corner cutter. If you don't have one, use a small disk. There are eight corners in total: four on the back and two each at the bottom of the front and flap.

Other than this, there is very little work needed on the back template, and it could be left out altogether. However, until you have a good understanding of design and cutting, it is better to have it than not.

6 With all three pieces cut and cornered, mark a stitch line along the top of the flap at 4 mm from the edge.

7 Now mark a 4 mm stitch line to the outside edge of the front piece.

8 If you now study the stitch lines of the front and flap, you will be able to understand the point made earlier about overlapping stitching. You can now see that if you stitch the flap to the front, you won't be able to fully stitch the sides because the flap will be in the way. Trying it the other way around doesn't help: if you stitch the sides first, you won't be able to stitch the flap in place.

This is where the rivets come into their own. You can stop the stitching short and use the rivets at about 3 mm from the edge to secure the corners in place. But to be precise, you need to know the size of the rivets.

The 14 g rivets used for this piece have 8 mm heads and 2.5 mm posts.

This means the center of the rivet hole from the edge needs to be 4 mm (the radius of the rivet) + 3 mm (the gap from the edge) = 7 mm. The next step, therefore, is to mark on our flap template the centers of the two rivet holes 7 mm down from the top and 7 mm in from each edge. I've also marked lines at 11 mm, showing the outer edges of the rivet. The center point is where I'll make the hole, and the outer mark is where I'll stop the stitching.

The holes will be punched once the item has been stitched together to ensure that everything lines up.

9 Starting with the flap, mark a row of stitching from the center line to the outer edge of each rivet. Get as close as you can without crossing this outer mark.

10 To ensure the stitching is symmetrical, add a line 10 mm in from the edge of the card at the corners to use as waypoints; this will help you line your holes up on both sides of the template.

11 Now mark a row of stitching on the front, from the center to the outer mark of the rivet on both sides of the card. Get as close as you can without crossing that mark.

12 Punch a 2.5 mm hole for each rivet at the center mark on the flap template.

13 Everything is now ready for you to cut the leather. Exactly as with the templates, cut a strip of leather 120 mm wide and 400 mm long. Then, having ensured you are working to a straight edge, measure your first cut, 170 mm, and then cut and continue until all three parts have been cut to size as in steps 3 and 4. Having done this, round the corners as in step 5.

14 Once the flap has been stitched into place, you will not be able to place the template on the front, so now is the time to mark and make the holes in the flap and front pieces.

First, mark the stitch and rivet holes on the flap. Remember that all the pieces will be stitched with the *grain* side facing front. You will glue and stitch these in stages.

15 Next, mark all the stitch holes on the front piece—but do not mark the rivet holes.

16 All edges not being stitched need dressing at this point. These are
• the bottom and sides of the flap
• the top of the back above the area where the front and flap pieces sit.

17 Once you have made all the necessary holes and dressed the edges, apply glue to the top of the flap and the top of the front piece where the flap is being stitched. Do not glue the outer edges, because these will need lifting to stitch the sides.

18 Glue the flap in place on the front. Mark the holes again with your irons and punch through both pieces.

19 Having made the holes, now stitch the top row and dress the top edge. Where the edges are not attached, pinch them together and treat them as one piece.

20 With the flap stitched to the front and dressed, glue the front to the back. Remember, all pieces should face the same way, grain side to the front.

With this glued into place, we can now punch the stitching holes through both pieces.

21 Once all the holes are made, stitch the front to the back. You will need to lift the flap slightly at the beginning and end to do this. Try not to stress the leather of the flap too much as you do it.

22 With all the pieces stitched together, only the corners are left unsecured. Take the 2.5 mm punch and—using the holes marked on the flap—punch through the final layer in both places.

23 To set these saddler's rivets, you will need two posts and two washers in 14 g, a rivet setter, a good set of snips, a maul or hammer, and a firm surface on which to strike.

24 Place the post into the hole from the back and lay it over a firm surface. I use a steel block. Place the washer over the post and then the hole of the setting tool over the post.

25 Tap down gently until the washer meets the leather. If you keep hitting it or hit it too hard, the washer will become lose and you will need to start again.

26 Now snip off the excess post with the cutters.

27 Take up the setter again, but this time place the dome over the cut post and hit firmly, turning the setter as you do so. Keep checking, and once the post has been domed and is smooth to the touch, it is done.

28 Finally, dress those edges of the leather not yet dressed, and your pocket protector is ready for use.

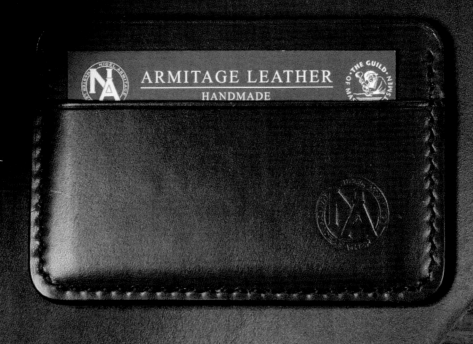

CARD HOLDER

When making something simple like a card holder, choose a leather that is firm, strong, and thin. A leather that is too soft can be hard to cut and pucker badly when stitched; too thick, and it can appear bulky. The leather needs to have a good resistance to being worked. As your skill grows, you will be able to use a broader range of leathers, but for now, let's keep it simple. A thin shoulder leather is ideal; something around 1–1.5 mm thick would be good to start with.

TOOLS & MATERIALS

Card for template	Sanding stick / detail
Rule	sander
Square	Needles—no. 4
Dividers	Thread—0.6 mm
Stitching or pricking	Stitching clam
irons—7 spi	Scissors or snips
Pulling block	Edger (beveler)
Maul or hammer	Slicker
Corner cutter, washer, or	Crease
coin	Edge Kote
French skive—12 mm	Beeswax

Case shoulder, 3–4 oz. (1.5 mm)

1 This card holder will have three openings: one central and two outer pockets. As with all our projects that are for a specific item, we need to know dimensions; in this case, a standard bank or credit card: 86 x 54 x 1 mm.

Very much like the notebook slip in Project 2, we are going to be using a 4 mm stitch line, so that same formula can be used with just a few minor adjustments.

The credit card is 1 mm thick, so adding this to our formula isn't vital if you want the pockets to take only one card. However, this project will allow two cards (a total of 2 mm) in each pocket, so the half-item-thickness measurement is included. The cards will be sitting horizontally (landscape).

Stitch line	4 mm	Constant
Stitch width	1 mm	Constant
Wiggle room	4 mm	Constant
Half item thickness	*1mm*	*Variable*
Item width	*86 mm*	*Variable*
Half item thickness	*1 mm*	*Variable*
Wiggle room	4 mm	Constant
Stitch width	1 mm	Constant
Stitch line	4 mm	Constant
Total	**106 mm**	

This means that the width of the card holder will be **106 mm**.

We now need to calculate the height of the body of the holder. This will be the height of the card, half the thickness, and our stitching calculation, plus how much we would like the leather to sit above the card, the cover.

Working from the top, the body formula will look like this:

Cover	10 mm	Constant
Item height	*54 mm*	*Variable*
Half item thickness	*1 mm*	*Variable*
Stitch width	1 mm	Constant
Stitch line	4 mm	Constant
Total	**70 mm**	

This gives us a total of **70 mm**.

2 One more calculation is needed: the height of the pocket. You will want enough of the card sticking out of the top of the pocket to be able to take hold of it to take it out. This is called "the pinch." Following our formula, the calculation should look like this:

Pinch	*10 mm*	*Variable*
Item height	*54 mm*	*Variable*
Half item thickness	*1 mm*	*Variable*
Stitch width	1 mm	Constant
Stitch line	4 mm	Constant
Total	**50 mm**	

This gives a measurement of **50 mm**.

Parts list:
The card holder is identical on both sides, so there are four pieces in total—two each for the body and pockets.

- 1, 2 Body x 2: 106 x 70 mm of 1.5 mm leather
- 3, 4 Pocket x 2: 106 x 50 mm of 1.5 mm leather

3

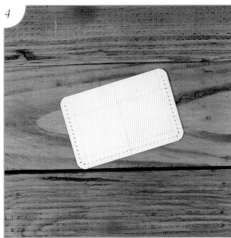

4

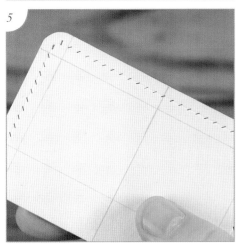

5

3 Now that you have the dimensions, cut a piece of card to the size of one of the body sections. Round all four corners—I've rounded mine using a 17 mm cutter.

Mark a center line and also a 50 mm line on the template to represent the height of the pocket.

Now add your stitch line to the base and each side of the template. This needs to end just before the top curve begins. The center opening will be used for cash or more cards, so if you stitch into the curve you'll reduce the size of the opening.

Set your rule stop to 10 mm and add a 10 mm line to the bottom and the two sides of the template. These way lines ensure your stitching is consistent on each side.

4 Begin marking your stitching holes on the template, ensuring the center hole crosses both the center line and stitch line. This is very important to achieve symmetrical stitching. From the center hole, work out and up on both sides, making sure the holes match the way lines on either side as you go.

5 You now need to look at where the stitching sits on the line that represents the top of the pocket. Ideally, the last hole at the top of the pocket is one stitch from the edge. However, if this hole is too close to the edge, it can tear the leather when used, so it's important to adjust the size of the pocket to suit the stitching. If the pocket has to be 1–2 mm shorter to accommodate this, it will make no difference to the overall finish.

6 You can see in the accompanying image that the 50 mm line (the top line) is too close to one of the stitching holes, but the second line below it fits nicely. This dictates that the height of the pocket must now change to 49 mm.

If you have to adjust the height of the pocket, make a note of it in your parts list so you do not get this wrong when cutting your leather.

7 You are now ready to cut your leather. First, you'll need to cut a strip of leather the width of the card holder. Referring to your parts list, you will need four pieces in total: two at 70 mm and two at 50 mm—so your strip of leather needs to be at least 240 mm (70 + 70 + 50 + 50) long and 106 mm wide. Allow a little more for mistakes and you should get all the necessary pieces from this, all at the same width.

When cutting, always cut your larger pieces first. If you make a mistake, a larger piece can become a smaller piece. The same cannot be said for the reverse.

8 With your parts cut, you are now ready to trim your corners. On the pockets, cut only the bottom two corners. On the two main body sections, cut all four corners.

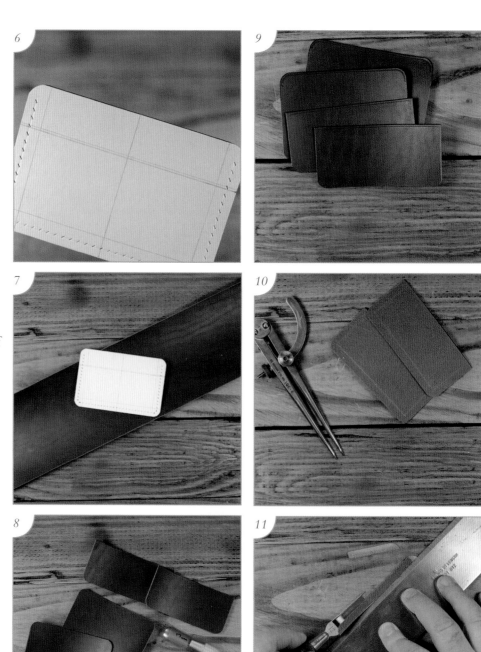

9 You don't have to mark and make all the stitching holes on each part: each pocket will be glued to a body section and treated as one piece.

First, however, the tops of the pockets need to be dressed. This would be more difficult to do if you waited until they were glued in place. Refer back to the edge-dressing section (see pp. 48–55) if you need guidance on this.

At the same time, dress the tops of the two bodies as well. You will need to dress only the top edge and both corners of these.

10 Once the pockets are dressed, the edges need to be thinned a little. If all four parts are put together, they total 6 mm, which can seem a little bulky.

To reduce this bulk, skive down the sides and bottoms of the pockets, using a 12 mm French skive. First, set the dividers to 6 mm and add a guide line to the back of the pockets.

11 Placing a rule on the guide line, push the French skive along the leather. Because half—6 mm—of the tool is off the leather, the tool cannot get to the front, so only half the thickness is taken off. This is enough to reduce the bulky look of the item.

12 Now rough up the leather on the body where the pocket will sit.

But do not mark above the height of the pocket, since this area will be visible once the pocket is set in place.

Next, glue one pocket to each body.

I use a contact glue to do this, but PVA, leather cement, and latex also work well.

13 You now have two parts, each consisting of a pocket glued to a body. Overlay the template, which has all the holes clearly marked.

Lightly mark through the template the end two holes of each straight row of stitching, all the holes on the corners, and three holes in the center.

14 Having done this, lightly add your 4 mm stitch line. If any of the holes you mark vary from the stitch line, always defer to the stitch line.

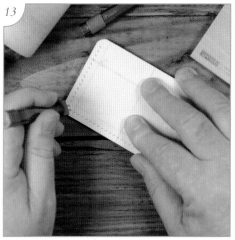

15 Mark and make your holes. If necessary, refer back to the section on stitching (see pp. 36–45) if you struggle. I explain there in some detail the double-pricking technique you need to use to make this item.

Once the holes have been made satisfactorily, you can glue both bodies together. If you do, don't be too enthusiastic with the glue; it can fill the holes. Let the glue cure properly—it will shrink back and should not impede your stitching too much.

16 If you are not confident with your hole marking, don't glue for now. Gluing is something you can work up to once your techniques become stronger. In the Slip Pouch project (see pp. 64–79), no glue was used and the edges look fine, but they can separate over time and with use, so it is something to work toward.

Whether you have used glue or not, you are now ready to stitch the two pieces together, using a stable clam to hold your item steady. Follow the instructions outlined in the section on stitching (see pp. 36–45).

17 Once they're stitched, use a bone folder to open up the seams. This will clear any glue that would otherwise prevent the cards from sitting properly.

18 Dress all unfinished edges and your item is ready for use.

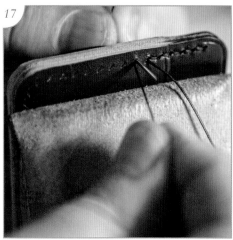

19

INTERMEDIATE PROJECTS

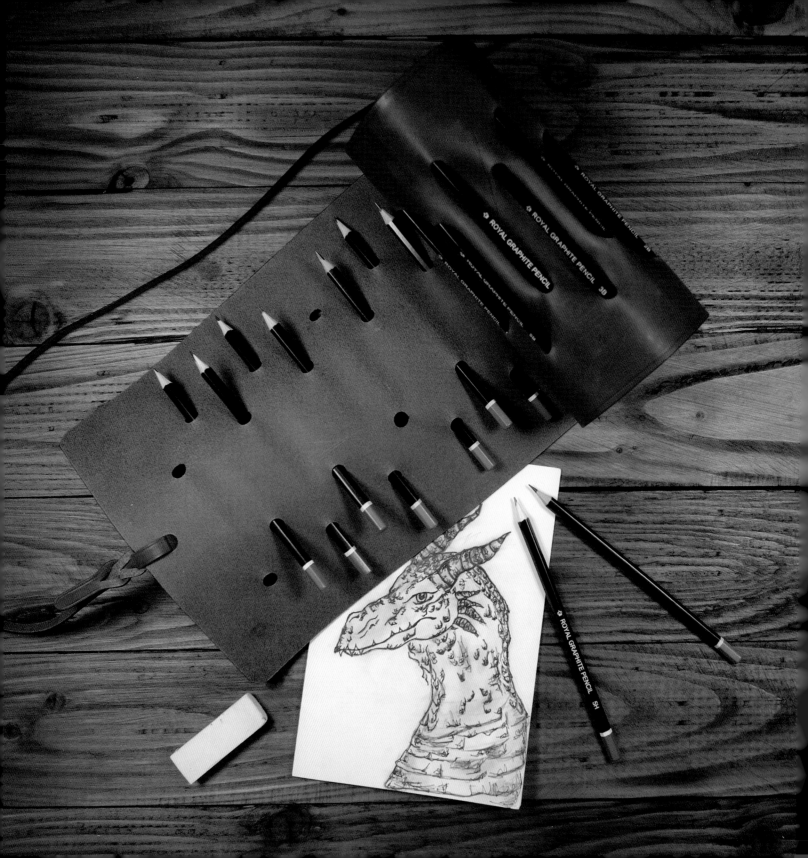

PENCIL ROLL

This is a stitch-free project and a really nice item to make. At first glance, it may look complex to follow, but it is simply a rectangle of leather with forty holes in it.

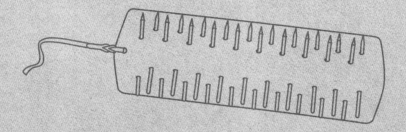

TOOLS & MATERIALS

Card for template	Hole punch—10 mm
Rule	Edger (beveler)
Square	Slicker
Dividers	Crease
Maul or hammer	Edge Kote
Corner cutter, washer,	Beeswax
or coin	

Case shoulder, 3–4 oz. (1.5 mm)

1a The holes are in four rows of ten, offset to allow twenty pencils to be held in place and rolled. The roll is finished with a simple 10 mm lace in the same leather and is attached with a bleed knot to secure it.

I have highlighted the two groups in different colors to make it clearer to see, and labeled the rows and columns.

About 80 percent of this project is the template. Take your time drawing it up, since one wrong line will cause your holes to be out of alignment.

1b To make the template you will need a good, stiff card 575 mm wide and 215 mm high. Each hole is 10 mm in diameter and is set 50 mm apart.

Rows 1 and 2 are separated and offset by 25 mm, as are rows 3 and 4.

1c Rather than writing a long list of measurements and instructions that may be confusing to follow, I've added a diagram showing the measurements and layout—once again, using two colors to make it clearer which hole goes where.

It's a good idea for you to do the same when marking your template; it might stop some confusion.

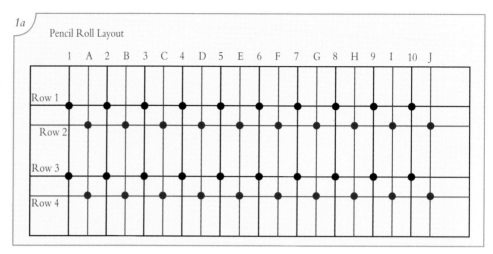

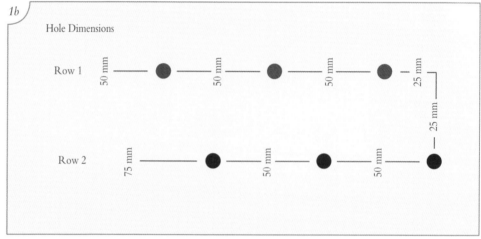

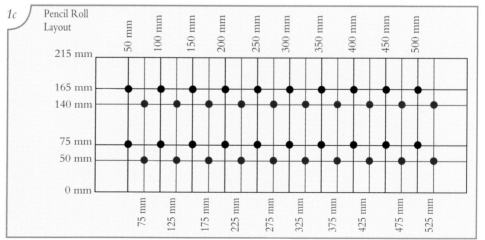

2 Cut your card—overall 575 x 215 mm. Then, using my layout instructions (1c), draw all the lines onto your card. Note that all my dimensions are taken from the bottom left corner.

Once the template is made, you will be able to repeat the project quite easily. Take your time with this template, since you may want to make more than one of these items, and repeating this process can be quite time consuming.

3 Once you have drawn all the lines in place, it is time to punch out all the holes.

Highlight each cross where a hole needs to be made. There are forty to punch out, and it is very easy to lose focus and punch a hole at the wrong intersection.

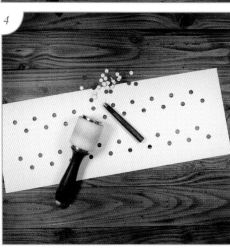

4 Once you have a clear indication of where the holes need to be, take your 10 mm hole punch and make all the holes in the template.

The lines drawn will act as reference points for the punch—sighting crosshairs if you will—and the more care you take with this, the better the leather will look.

The completed template should look something like this.

5 At one end we need to mark a short center line, 107.5 mm from either side. Ensure both lines meet up.

6 On this line, mark 20 mm in from the edge of the leather. Make another 10 mm hole on this cross. This will be the hole you use to secure your lace.

7 The template is complete. You are ready to cut the leather—here, a piece of 1.5 mm Lyveden shoulder.

The lace needs to be 10 mm wide and 800 mm long. Cut this first to make sure you get the length. We will come back to it later.

Next, cut your leather to the same size as the template: 575 mm wide and 215 mm high.

8 Line up the template with the leather so it is square and all edges are flush. If you have some heavy weights, hold down the template with them now.

9 With the weights in place, punch through each hole of the template until all forty-one holes have been made.

The difficult bit is now over. All that is left to do is to dress the edges of the leather.

You can leave the corners square or slightly round them; I round mine with a 21 mm corner punch, but this is your choice—both options work.

You need to add a crease, then bevel, slick, and coat the edges.

The final task is to add the lace, first rounding the ends to finish them off nicely.

Dress the edges; bevel, slick, and coat. I added a crease, but it is a thin, narrow lace and difficult to keep still when creasing. If you are not yet confident in this technique, do not add one. If you are up to the task, hold the lace against a rule to keep it straight.

10 The lace is attached to the roll by using a bleed knot.

First, cut two 20 mm long slots in the leather: one 25 mm from one end of the lace, and the other 95 mm from the same end. It should look like this, with the two slots 50 mm apart.

11 To tie the knot, hold the leather grain side up at the end with the holes. Place the short end into the hole. Now pull it back on itself and push it through the second slot.

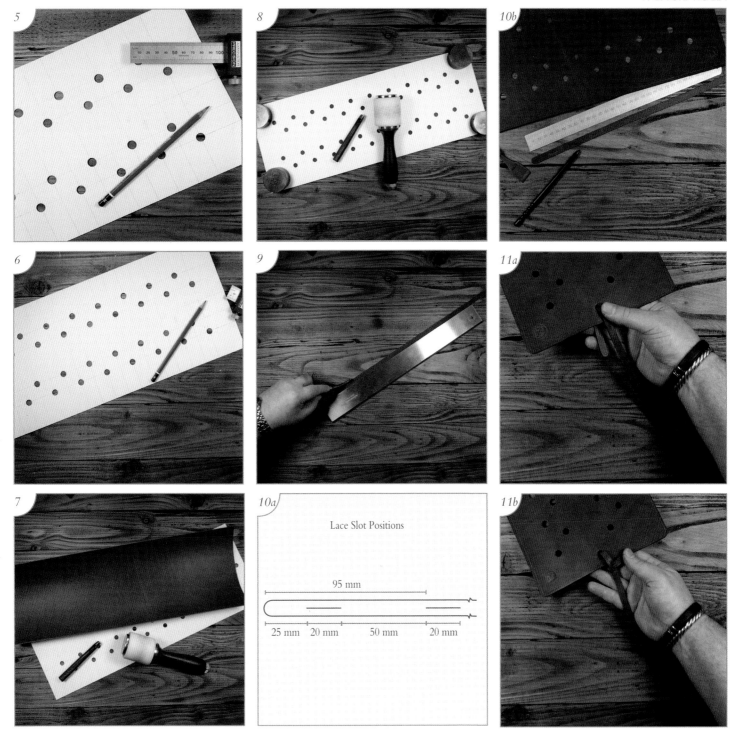

5

6

7

8

9

10a

Lace Slot Positions

95 mm

25 mm   20 mm   50 mm   20 mm

10b

11a

11b

12 Twist the leather in the hole to flatten in.

13 Now take the other end of the leather and pull it through the first slot.

14 Pull it all the way through and then twist it until flat. It may take a little working in to tighten up the knot and get it to sit flat, but once done, it should look like this.

You are now ready to load up your pencil roll and enjoy using it.

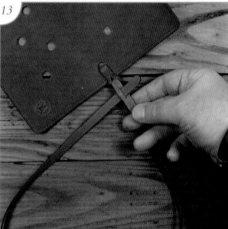

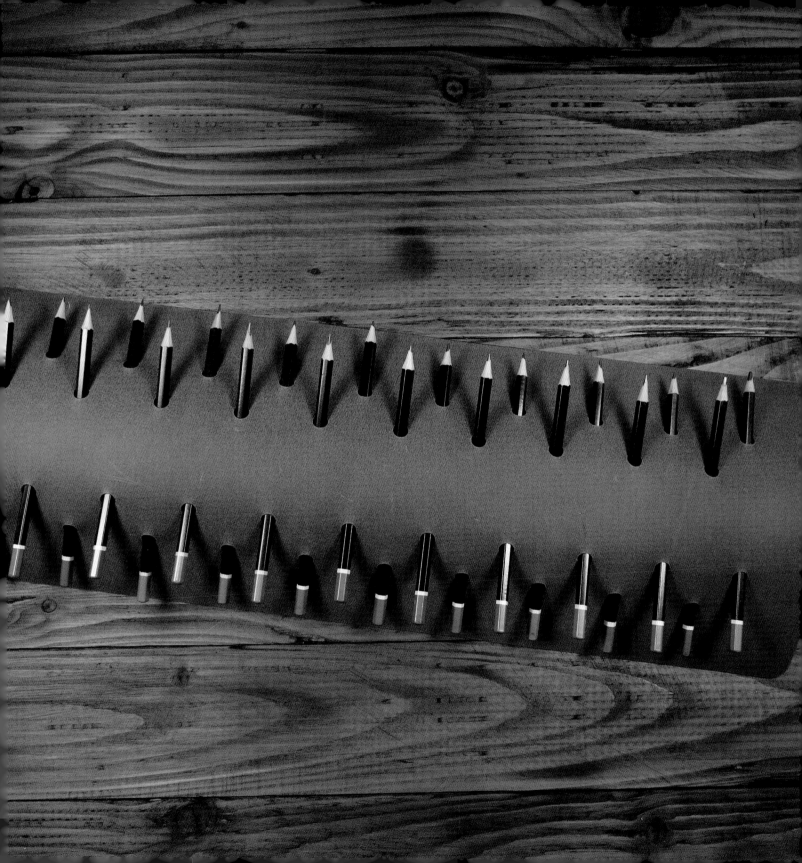

ARMITAGE LEATHER
HANDMADE LEATHER TOOLS
The Iron Pulling Block

MADE IN BRITAIN

www.armitageleather.com
www.just2wood.org

STITCHING-IRON POUCH

As with all the other projects in this book, this is an ideal building block in your leathercrafting journey, and a great way to look after your tools. It's made of three pieces: the back, which folds over to the front, ending in a flap; a pocket; and a strap into which the flap tucks.

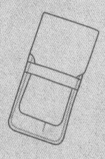

TOOLS & MATERIALS

Card for template	Sanding stick / detail
Rule	sander
Square	Needles—no. 4
Dividers	Thread—0.6 mm
Stitching or pricking	Stitching clam
irons—8 spi	Scissors or snips
Pulling block	Edger (beveler)
Maul or hammer	Slicker
Corner cutter, washer,	Crease
or coin	Edge Kote
	Beeswax

Case shoulder, 6–7 oz. (2.5 mm)

1 This project is to make the case for a pair of stitching irons—the ones I'll be using to make the case.

2 As always, we now need to work out the dimensions, but since these tools are an odd shape, it's easy to get lost trying to follow their outlines. To keep things simple, treat each tool as a rectangle, working to their outer dimensions.

Eight-tooth iron
Width	34 mm
Height	120 mm
Depth	8 mm

Two-tooth iron
Width	13 mm
Height	120 mm
Depth	8 mm

These dimensions—and knowing we are working to rectangles—provide the building blocks for the design. You can always add to these, but it is a good way to get started.

The outer stitch line is going to be 4 mm from the edge of the leather, but unlike earlier projects, you don't need to allow for the 1 mm stitch width since neither tool actually sits against the stitching. The width of the eight-tooth tool is 34 mm. There is no edge to add, since the two-tooth pocket will sit next to this one, but you do not want the tools touching, so add another 2 mm, bringing us to 40 mm—4 mm + 34 mm + 2 mm.

The two-tooth iron is much narrower, but if we leave the width of this pocket at 13 mm plus the 4 mm for the stitching, it would be too tight, so more calculation is needed. The width of the shaft, which will sit in the pocket, is actually only 10 mm, and the thickness is 8 mm, so you don't need to add very much—say 6 mm—to either side to open the pocket up. This gives figures of 6 mm + 10 mm + 6 mm + 4 mm = 26 mm.

Putting the two dimensions together gives a pocket width of 66 mm, with three rows of stitching—one on either side set in 4 mm from the edge, and a third row 40 mm in to separate the pocket into two sections.

As to the pocket's height: the length of the shaft to the bottom of the head of both irons is 80 mm. If you add to this 6 mm to help with the thickness, plus the 4 mm stitch line, this means the pocket will be 90 mm high.

3 Next, the back section and flap.
Starting at the bottom, the measurements are 4 mm stitch line + 6 mm space for the thickness + 120 mm for the height of the tools = 130 mm from the bottom of the pouch to the top of the tools. The leather has to bend over the tools, but this must not be too tight a fold—the tools will cut the leather if it is. Allow 10 mm to prevent this.

Next question: How far should the flap come down the front? This very much depends on the closure. Here, a strap of leather traps the flap. This strap needs to

2

Pocket

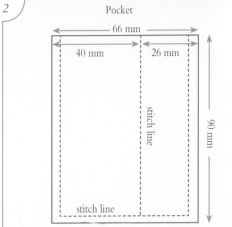

66 mm

40 mm   26 mm

stitch line

90 mm

stitch line

3

Flap

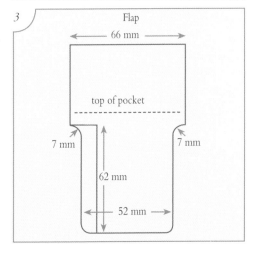

66 mm

top of pocket

7 mm   7 mm

62 mm

52 mm

sit quite deep, so I've allowed 110 mm—so, 20 mm from the bottom.

These dimensions added together give a final measurement for the back of 130 mm + 10 mm + 110 mm = 250 mm.

The final piece to consider before the final parts list is the strap, the strip of leather to hold the flap down. This will be the width of the pouch—66 mm—but once the tools are inside, this would be a little too tight, so add 2 mm just to lift it slightly; 12 mm will be sufficient for the height.

Now we have a parts list:

1. Back   66 x 250 mm
2. Pocket   66 x 90 mm
3. Strap   68 x 12 mm

The final design feature to be considered before making the templates is tapering the flap.

Even with the addition of the extra 2 mm to the strap, a 66 mm wide flap would be difficult to get in and out of a 68 mm strap. The answer is to reduce the edges a little, 7 mm either side, below the line of the top of the pocket.

So the taper will be 62 mm long, and the strap will sit just below where the flap tapers, 74 mm from the bottom of the pouch.

4 It is now time to cut all the templates. Working to the parts list, cut all three sections from stiff card and add a center line.

First, the front. Curve the bottom two corners and add a 4 mm stitch line. Then set your rule stop to 10 mm and add the three way lines, one to the bottom and one on either side.

Add another stitch line 40 mm from the left side of the card.

Starting at the bottom in the center, work out and up, adding your holes following the stitch line and making sure you hit the way lines at the same points on both sides of the card.

For the dividing line of stitching, start at the top and put the first hole one stitch from the end of the card, working down toward the bottom but stopping two or three stitch lengths from the bottom stitch line.

5 Next template to prepare is for the back and flap. You will be adding the holes based on the front template, so this one is mainly for the cutting.

First, curve the back two corners to match the front. Next, mark the taper height on the flap end at 62 mm.

Set the rule stop to 7 mm, and at the flap end mark two 7 mm lines on either side (compare with photo 3). Using a corner cutter or disk, cut a curve where the 7 mm lines meet the 62 mm line to round them on the inside. Trim off the remaining length and then round off the corners at the flap end.

6 You don't really need a strap template, but cut it to add to your set for future use.

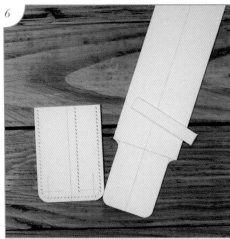

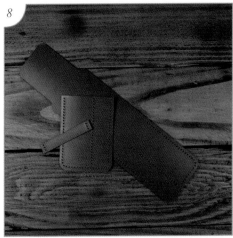

7 With all the templates cut, holed and marked, we are ready to cut the leather. The common measurement here is 66mm, so cut a strip of leather 66mm wide and long enough to get both pieces out of it, so at least 380mm.

Using the back template, apply all cuts to the flap to achieve the taper.

8 Using the front template, mark the beginning and end holes of all straight rows of stitching and all corner holes. Add a 4mm stitch line and if any of the holes are drifting off the line, defer to the line.

Using the front template, apply the holes to the back piece. You can, if you wish, glue everything together and punch through all the leather at once, but in my experience your stitching will not look as good if you do so.

When you come to the holes for the dividing line, it's very important that *you turn the template over* to ensure the holes are on the right side.

Finally, cut your 68mm x 12mm strap and add a 4mm stitch line to the two ends. Then marking one stitch in from the top edge, add your holes.

To make the strap sit a little better, skive the inside of the ends slightly. This will remove a bit of bulk and make the edges look a little sleeker where they sit on the leather.

9 With all parts cut and all holes made, dress the top of the pocket, the flap, and either side of the strap.

10 You are now ready to stitch. Start with the dividing line. You will not be able to stitch this once the strap is in place, so the dividing line is the first row to take care of.

11 Once you have stitched this, put the strap in place. It should lie 74mm from the bottom of the pouch. Line it up with a rule and then line it up to the closest hole.

Count how many holes are above it, on mine there are five holes. When stitching, ensure you have five holes above the strap on both sides so it will be straight.

12 With everything in place, stitch your outer line. Once stitched dress your edge and you are done.

10

11

12

PASSPORT COVER

While this project is focused on a passport, change the dimensions and it becomes a notebook or book cover—even a document folio if you make it large enough.

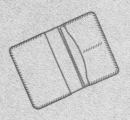

TOOLS & MATERIALS

Card for template

Rule

Square

Dividers

Stitching or pricking
 irons—7 spi

Pulling block

Maul or hammer

Corner cutter, washer,
 or coin

French skive—12 mm

Sanding stick / detail
 sander

Needles—no. 4

Thread—0.6 mm

Stitching clam

Scissors or snips

Edger (beveler)

Slicker

Crease

Edge Kote

Beeswax

Case shoulder, 3–4 oz. (1.5 mm)

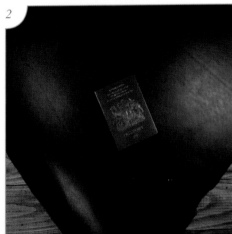

1 Before starting to design this item, you need to decide on some important information:

a. The dimensions of the passport— width, height, thickness
b. What thickness of leather to use
c. How many pockets it will have
d. What the cover will be used for— passport, cards, tickets, etc.
e. At what distance from the edge the stitch line should be

Having all this information at hand before beginning makes designing the cover much easier.

Let's begin with the dimensions of the passport. Remember to always record width first, then height, and then thickness or depth. I believe passports are much the same size, but check yours. The dimensions should be close to

a. 88 x 125 x 4 mm

2 What thickness of leather to use? This is a good question, since you may not have access to the same leather I am using. The leather needs to be thin enough so that the item is usable, but thick enough so it is not floppy or weak.

b. Lamport case shoulder, 3–4 oz. (1.5 mm) thick

3 Next, decide how many pockets it will have—one to hold the passport, one opposite to take tickets, and two on top of this to hold cards.

c. This cover will have three layers of pockets at 1.5 mm thickness each, giving a total thickness of 4.5 mm—but let's round this up to 5 mm.

4 Deciding what to put in your cover is a personal choice and one for you to ponder. This one has a passport, tickets, and business cards. This may not seem important, but it is: we need to have an idea of the amount of additional thickness to be added to the cover.

d. Passport (4 mm), tickets (1 mm), six business cards per pocket at 4 mm

5 Finally, what stitch line will be used? This can change from item to item and is often influenced by how many stitches per inch (spi) are used.

I have chosen 7 spi since this is a good all-around spi and very forgiving if you are just getting started. Using 7 spi means that the stitch line wants to be quite close, and you should use a fine 0.4 mm thread.

e. 4 mm, 7 spi, 0.4 mm thread

Taking time to gather this information at the outset helps in the design of the cover. It will have one pocket for the passport on the right and two pockets for tickets and cards on the left, with these all being stitched to a body stretching across the full width.

This means that our cover will be made of four pieces of leather, and you now need to determine the dimensions of those pieces.

Start with the width, working left to right. The first measurement is the

stitch line (4 mm), plus an additional 1 mm for the width of the stitch, since this will have an impact on the internal measurements.

The next measurement is the width of the passport—88 mm.

The next is the spine, the bend of the leather needing to be the overall thickness of everything that will go inside the cover:

Pockets x 3	5 mm (3c)
Passport	4 mm (4d)
Tickets	1 mm (4d)
Business cards	4 mm (4d)

This gives us a total of 14 mm for the bend. This figure will allow the leather to fold over so the outer edges meet correctly. If you don't add enough, the cover won't fold properly. If you add too much, the cover will be floppy and the edges will sit unevenly.

Now to the other side of the cover, which is the same in reverse: 88 mm for

the passport +1 mm for the stitching and 4 mm for the stitch line.

These numbers identify the width of the body of the cover as 20 mm and are shown laid out in diagram **5a**.

The height is next. It is worked out in a very similar fashion to the width, except that the passport will need wiggle room to allow it to slide in and out of the cover easily. Adding 2 mm of wiggle room to either side gives these measurements:

Stitch line	4 mm
Stitching	1 mm
Wiggle room	2 mm
Passport	125 mm
Wiggle room	2 mm
Stitching	1 mm
Stitch line	4 mm
Total	**139 mm**

This gives a total of 139 mm, but for ease, round this up to 140 mm: a little more wiggle room can't hurt.

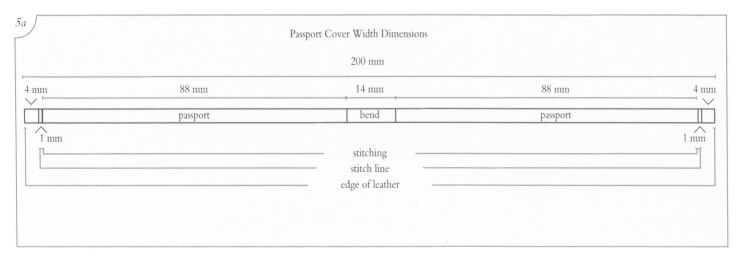

5a

Passport Cover Width Dimensions

200 mm

4 mm   88 mm   14 mm   88 mm   4 mm

passport   bend   passport

1 mm   1 mm

stitching
stitch line
edge of leather

5b

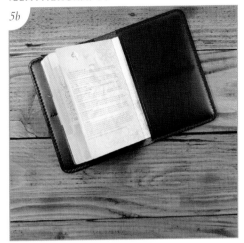

6

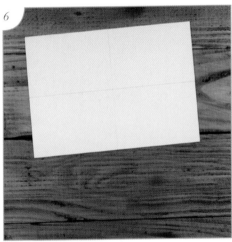

7

Next the large pockets need to be calculated. These will be the same height as the body—140 mm. As far as the width is concerned, the passport is 88 mm wide. The leather inside needs to stop short of the spine so the passport can close. Removing 8 mm will be enough; the stitch line and stitching of 4 mm + 1 mm need to be added, bringing the width of the pocket to a total of 85 mm.

6 Finally, on to the card pockets.
Again, the height will be the same as the large pockets, 140 mm. The width is determined by how much pinch you want showing. The width (landscape measurement) of the cards is 86 mm; this is how they will sit in the pocket (see photo on p. 113).

Allowing 20 mm of the card exposed for the pinch, this gives a measurement of 66 mm. Adding the stitch line (4 mm) and space for stitching (1 mm) will total 71 mm—call it 70 mm for ease of measurement.

Now we have a parts list:

1. Body   200 x 140 mm
2. Large pocket   85 x 140 mm
3. Large pocket   85 x 140 mm
4. Card pocket   70 x 140 mm

Once you are experienced, a template won't be necessary for each piece—the body with all the pockets marked in place will suffice. For now, however, you should create three templates: one for the body, one for the two large pockets, and one for the card pocket.

First, the body. This needs to be drawn up and cut first because it may lead to a minor adjustment to the pockets.

Begin by cutting a stiff piece of card to the size of the body, and draw a center line both horizontally and vertically to the body section.

7 Using the measurements for the large pockets, add a fine line to the template on either side of the center line, showing where they will sit. Do this lightly, since this measurement may change.

Do the same for the measurement of the card pocket on the left-hand side of the template.

This may be a sensible moment to add an arrow or mark the word "TOP" to your template to avoid any confusion later on.

8 Round the corners—I used a 21 mm corner cutter. Note that all four corners of the body need to be rounded, but when it's time to cut the pocket templates, only one side of the large pocket and the card pocket will be rounded. The opening will be left square.

9 To prepare for the stitching, add the 4 mm stitch line to the edge of the template where it will be stitched.

The lines added for the large pockets will be where the stitch line starts and stops.

Add the holes by starting at the point where the center line crosses the stitch line. Your first hole should be centered to this point.

Adding the holes in this fashion is a more accurate way to ensure your holes line up, but it can still be difficult, especially if you drift off the lines. A nice tip to help you keep on track is to add way lines or markers to your template. Here, I have added three extra lines 10 mm in from each edge of the card, either side, and on the base.

As you go around the corners, you will see if the holes are the same distance from the lines on the right as they are on the left, thus ensuring a good symmetry.

10 With the center line, stitch line, and way-lines marked, it's time to begin adding the holes.

Starting from the center line, add your holes to the stitch line as accurately as possible, first working out and up to the left, then repeating on the right.

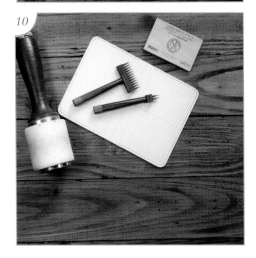

11 By adding the holes to the templates first, you can see clearly where all your holes will end in relation to the edges of the pockets.

What you are trying to do is ensure the last hole at the opening is one full stitch from the edge of the leather.

It's important to remember that if you are using different irons from the ones I'm using, your adjustments may be different from mine.

If you have added your holes correctly and the lines do not sit quite right, the size of the pockets can be adjusted to suit. Either way, once you have confirmed that you have the correct size or have made an adjustment to suit, you are ready to cut the templates for the pockets.

First cut a template for the large pocket. This can be used twice. Next cut another for the card pocket.

Round off only the corners that will sit at the outer edge, and repeat the process for adding your holes—the same as it was for the body.

12 If you are feeling confident, you can at this point add a nice curve at the top of the card pocket—a design feature you can play with to make the cover design uniquely your own.

I have added a large scallop covering both pockets, but you can add one to each or leave the pocket flat.

13 Finally, the card pocket will need a row of stitching in the center to separate it into two individual pockets.

On the card pocket template, add a row of holes to the center line, but stopping short of the opening and the existing stitch line. Do this after you have added your detailing—if any—to the opening.

14 Once you've made all the holes, you'll be able to see how precise you are. If you can line up the holes in all three templates, this is a good indicator of your accuracy and bodes well for the leather.

15 You are now ready to cut the leather, working to the parts list. First, ensure you have incorporated any new dimensions if you have had to adjust them, then cut the four sections needed from your desired leather.

Precision is the key here; the more precise you are, the better everything will line up.

Remember, we are prepricking our holes, so take your time—measure twice, cut once.

Once the parts have been cut to shape and the appropriate corners rounded, we are ready to add the stitch lines.

You need to do this in the correct order. First, add the stitching holes to the body. Take the template and lay it over the body, ensuring it is centered and flush on all sides. It is sensible to hold it in place with a weight.

16 Turn the template landscape for this procedure. Take a two-pronged iron and mark the following holes:

- For the left-hand line, the two holes at the top and bottom of the straight run
- For the right-hand line, the two holes at the top and bottom of the straight run
- For the bottom line, the two holes at the left and right of the straight run
- For the corners, all holes on the curve

Keep the tool perfectly vertical. If it leans, the holes will be out of line. If they have missed the stitch line, defer to the line when making the holes.

17 Remove the template from the leather, add a stitch line between the marks, and make all of the holes in the body.

At the ends of each line, the top two holes should line up with the top two holes on the large pockets.

Now, add one more hole to each side. This will cause the stitching to sit over the edge of the leather at the opening of the pocket, making it a little stronger and helping it sit flat.

After you have made the holes, the gap between the stitching is now clearly indicated.

This area will need dressing before the cover is stitched together, since it will be a little hard to bevel these edges and dress them nicely once stitched.

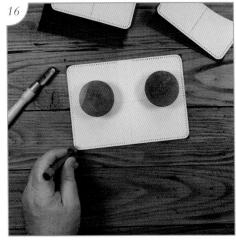

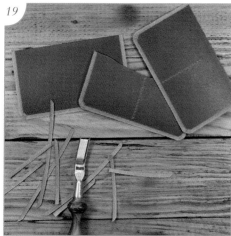

18 While dressing these two edges, also dress the tops of the three pockets with your desired crease, bevel, and Edge Kote, since this will also be hard to do once stitched.

19 Before making any holes on the pockets, we need to give a little thought to the edges of the cover.

To the left, there will be three layers of leather—almost 5 mm thick—which can make the item look a little chunky. A nice way to deal with this is to skive a little leather off the back of each pocket. Even if you take only 0.5 mm, it will make a big difference.

I use a 12 mm wide French skive to do this. Marking a 5 mm line on the back of the leather gives a line to follow less than half the width of the tool. Cutting the leather on the flat will cause the blade to overhang by 7 mm. This ensures I don't cut into the leather too deeply, and will leave about 1 mm of leather behind.

This is a very clean way of achieving a rather narrow skive.

20 After all the edges of the pockets have been skived, on one of the large pockets, mark where the card pocket will sit, and rough this area for gluing. Be careful not to damage the leather above this mark, since it will be visible.

Using a glue of your choice—here I used impact glue since it bonds well and remains flexible—glue the card pocket to the large pocket.

Once you have done this, lay the card pocket template over the card pocket and carefully line it up. Through the template, mark the holes for the center row of stitching. Remove the template and punch the holes through both pieces of leather. When you have made these holes, stitch the two pieces together. Once this is done, the card pocket and the large pocket can be treated as one piece of leather.

21 Take the large pocket template and lay over one of the two pockets. As you did with the body, mark the ends of all three straight lines of stitching and all the holes on the curves. Repeat for the other pocket.

Having added these marks, run a stitch line around and fully make all the holes. Again, defer to the line if you have any variation.

22 The cover can now be stitched together. If you aren't yet confident about your holes, stitch it without gluing it first: the slight skive will cause the edges to pull together still giving you a nice edge. If you are confident, however, a bead of glue can't hurt—not too much as you do not want to fill the holes with glue.

Once you're ready, stitch both pockets into place.

All that is left is to dress the edges. A light sand first will even up any misalignment—you are now ready for your next journey overseas!

BELT

A belt is probably the most utilitarian piece of leather we own. It keeps our pants up; is a platform for carrying pouches, sheaths, and the like; and is a fashion statement.

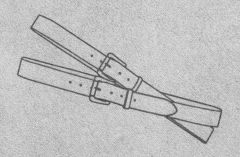

TOOLS & MATERIALS

Card for template	Buckle— 1½ in.
Rule	Keep—1½ in.
Square	Corner cutter, washer,
Dividers	or coin
Stitching or pricking	Needles—no. 4
irons—7 spi	Thread—0.6 mm
Pulling block	Stitching clam
Maul or hammer	Scissors or snips
Crew/oblong	Edger (beveler)
punch—1½ in.	Slicker
Strap end	Crease
punch—1½ in.	Edge Kote
Hole punch—6 mm	Beeswax

Bridle butt, 8–9 oz. (3.5 mm)

1 This is a belt to use with jeans, with a brass buckle and a brass keep. It's 38 mm (1½ in.) wide, so a strong leather is best because it is less likely to stretch or misshape. A fashion belt, however, can be made with a softer and more supple leather. Two types of leather that we could use for a belt are bridle butt and shoulder.

Bridle butt is usually found 4–6 mm thick. It's stuffed full of waxes and oils when it's being made, making it dense, firm, and less prone to stretch.

Shoulder is easy to work and easy to finish and looks very nice with little effort. It's a softer leather than bridle and is prone to stretch under tension, especially if it gets wet. It's ideal for a fashion belt that's going to be worn loose.

Before starting, it's important to understand how to measure a belt and how it is supposed to sit. The best way to measure for a new belt is to measure an existing one!

First, while the belt is being worn,

take note of the hole being used. Remove the belt and measure from that hole to the point where the prong meets the bar on the buckle.

If you have only a waist size to work with, remember that the measurement of your waist is not the same as the length of a belt. A belt is worn over a number of layers of clothing, so it has to travel farther—make it longer.

The first belt loop on a decent pair of pants or jeans tends be 150 mm from the center. The belt needs to extend far enough so its end sits comfortably in that loop and doesn't slip out of the flap—an extra 50 mm will do. In view of this, try to keep at least 200 mm between the center hole and the end of the belt.

Nine holes for a belt, with the fifth being the center hole, is a forgiving number to start with, giving more flexibility if you make a slight mistake with the measuring. As you get better, this can be dropped to seven or even five—but if you do reduce the number of holes, be sure to still maintain that

200 mm distance.

There will be two templates for the belt, one for each end—the billet and the buckle. Making the templates in two parts means they can be adjusted when measuring the strap for the belt.

First, the template for the buckle end. You will need some thick stiff card—I used 1.5 mm thick mount board. Cut two strips 38 mm wide and 350 mm long.

The sketch below shows the buckle template laid out with the stitching, gaps for the keep, and a slot for the buckle prong—the movable bar of the buckle that goes through the hole.

The gaps allow for the addition of a metal keep and make stitching the belt much easier.

To ensure accuracy, all the holes in this project will be prepicked with nine-tooth and five-tooth irons in 7 spi, punching all the way through to open the holes up. You may use whatever irons you have, but keep to the twelve- and five-hole ratio. The distance between the end of the slot and the end of the leather, in my case 85 mm, does not matter.

This may change for you if you use different irons, but it will still work as long as you achieve the correct symmetry.

Using this process requires no initial measurements, since the stitching sets these out as we go. We know that it will need a 20 mm gap for the keep and a 38 mm slot for the buckle, but these

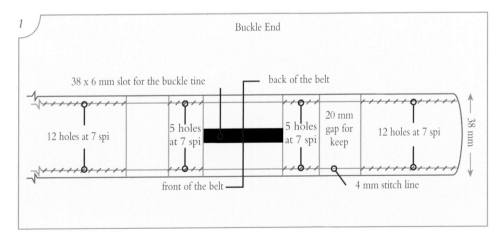

1

Buckle End

38 x 6 mm slot for the buckle tine

back of the belt

12 holes at 7 spi

5 holes at 7 spi

5 holes at 7 spi

20 mm gap for keep

12 holes at 7 spi

38 mm

front of the belt

4 mm stitch line

are added as the holes are marked out.

2 Starting at one end, slightly round your template. You can leave it straight if you wish, but it is a neat way to finish the back of your belt. Now add two stitch lines, 4 mm from the edge of the card on either side.

3 You need to add to your template the stitch holes and spaces outlined in sketch 1; namely, 12 holes—20 mm gap, 5 holes—38 mm gap, 5 holes— 20 mm gap, 12 holes.

Working from right to left, place one tooth of the long iron over the edge of the card and begin to mark your first set of holes. This will ensure that the last hole is one full stitch from the end of the leather.

4 Mark and make your first row of twelve holes. Having done this, mark a line at the end of this row and a second line 20 mm farther on. This will

be your keep gap. Most keeps tend to be about 12.5 mm (0.5 in.), so 20 mm should be enough, but check yours before you move forward, and adjust if needed.

5 After the 20 mm gap, add another five holes and draw a further line at the end these.

You have now reached the point where you need to add the slot for the prong. How long should it be? A rough rule of thumb is that the length of the slot reflects the width of the belt—so in this case, 38 mm. Mark a line at the end of the five holes, and another 38 mm farther on.

You will need to know where the center of the bend is, so a line in the middle of this space is also needed.

This completes the back section. Now move to the front, repeating the mirror image of what you have just done.

The leather will bend around, centered in the middle of the slot, so the front needs to reflect the back.

At the line marked for the end of the slot, add five holes and mark a line at the end of the row. Mark a second line 20 mm farther on, and after this, twelve more holes.

Repeat this for the other side of the template; the lines will now act as a guide.

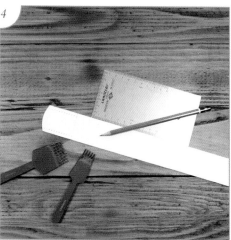

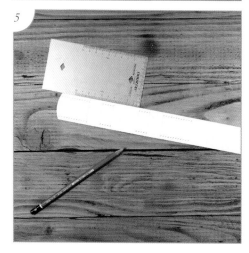

6 The next task is to add the 38 mm slot between the two marked lines. It can be added with a crew punch—also known as an oblong or bag punch—or can also be made using a 6 mm hole punch. Make two holes 38 mm apart and then carefully cut between the holes with a knife.

Here I used a crew punch, setting the punch in the center of the template between the two marks and punching through.

7 There is one more mark you need to add to this template: a point from which you can measure when you start working on the leather.

Most 38 mm buckles tend to be almost square, so we need a measurement of 38 mm from the center of the slot toward the back of the belt.

This mark represents where the buckle prong sits on the bar and where it meets the center hole of the belt when worn. The diagram (**7b**) shows the outline of a buckle and where this hole should sit.

8 With the template for the buckle end taken care of, the next step is to look at the billet end.

In most cases, the distance between the first hole and the end of the belt is about 100 mm, with the distance between the holes being 25 mm. The number of holes needs to be uneven so the buckle can be centered when worn.

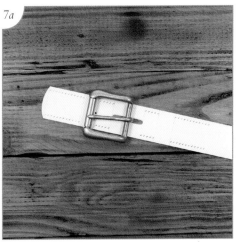

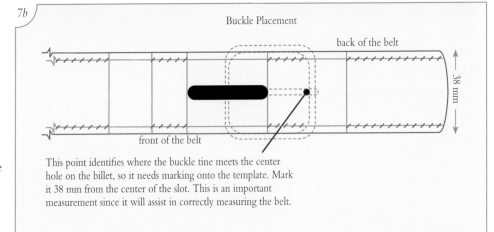

Buckle Placement

back of the belt

38 mm

front of the belt

This point identifies where the buckle tine meets the center hole on the billet, so it needs marking onto the template. Mark it 38 mm from the center of the slot. This is an important measurement since it will assist in correctly measuring the belt.

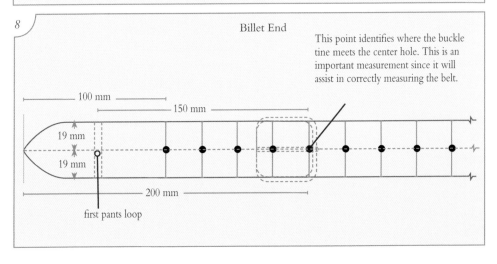

Billet End

This point identifies where the buckle tine meets the center hole. This is an important measurement since it will assist in correctly measuring the belt.

100 mm

150 mm

19 mm

19 mm

200 mm

first pants loop

These are very loose rules and can be adjusted to suit your own needs, size, and style.

As mentioned, errors can be made when measuring a belt, so work with nine holes to give an additional margin for error.

Decide on the design you want for the belt tip. I have chosen an English point.

Mark 100 mm from the tip and draw a line. Continue on, drawing eight more lines 25 mm apart.

Finally, draw a center line 19 mm from the edges of the card to create a center line running the length of the card.

Your belt holes will be at the points where the lines cross.

9 Take a hole punch big enough to fit over the tine of the buckle.

10 Punch all the holes in the template.

11 Both templates are now complete. Producing them is by far the most time-consuming part of making a belt. However, once a good template has been made, it doesn't have to be made again.

Added to this, when you take the template to the strap, there will be no guesswork, no working out measurements on the leather, and no marking the leather unnecessarily—it will come together rather easily, as you will see next.

We are now ready to cut the leather. You will need a strip 38 mm wide. If you are using bridle leather, it is likely to be just over 1.5 meters (60 in.) long.

Don't cut the strap to length! If the strap is too long, leave it so. Most mistakes are made at the buckle end, and if you have already cut the strap to length and make a mistake, you have nowhere to go. If you have left it too long, you have a chance to redeem yourself.

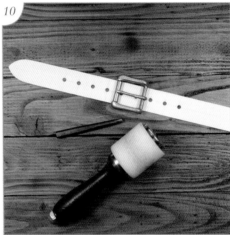

12 First, lay the template for the buckle end over the strap. If you are able to hold it down with some weights, even better.

13 The hardest thing to get right is the slot: mark this first. Place the crew punch over the template and give a single firm strike to mark the leather.

Remove the template and ensure the slot is straight. If it is, replace the crew punch without the template and strike through. If this works, you can move forward. If, however, it has twisted and is off line, you have potentially wasted only 125 mm of leather, so you can cut the error off and try again.

14 Once you have successfully made the slot, replace the template, lining up with the edges of the strap and slot. Now mark lightly with a scratch awl the first and last hole of each row of holes. There is potential to go off line, so do not mark too deeply.

This is also a good opportunity to mark the end of the strap if you intend to round it.

15 When marked up, remove the template and run two stitch lines— still at 4 mm—down the edges of the strap between the first and last holes of all the rows. Do not go beyond this, since this area will be taken care of with a crease line.

It is possible that the holes you made with the scratch awl do not quite sit on the stitch lines you just made. When punching the holes, always defer to the stitch line; the marks will tell you where the holes need to be on the line, but ensure the irons are on the line when you punch through.

16 Now punch your stitch holes into the leather.

At this point the wisdom of having made two templates becomes apparent.

When you measured your belt, you will have recorded the measurement: let's call it 34 inches to use as an example. Lay the strap out flat and place the buckle template over the buckle end of the strap.

Place a long rule next to the strap, with the end of the rule or 0 at the small measuring hole on the template.

17 Now place the billet template onto the strap so the center hole lines up with 34 inches.

18 Hold down the template with weights so you can mark the holes and the end of the strap for cutting.

Using this process will ensure the correct length belt every time— provided your waist measurements are right.

19 Cut the strap end and make all your holes. The strap is almost a belt.

20 If you are able, skiving down the back of the belt is a good idea to remove some of the bulk.

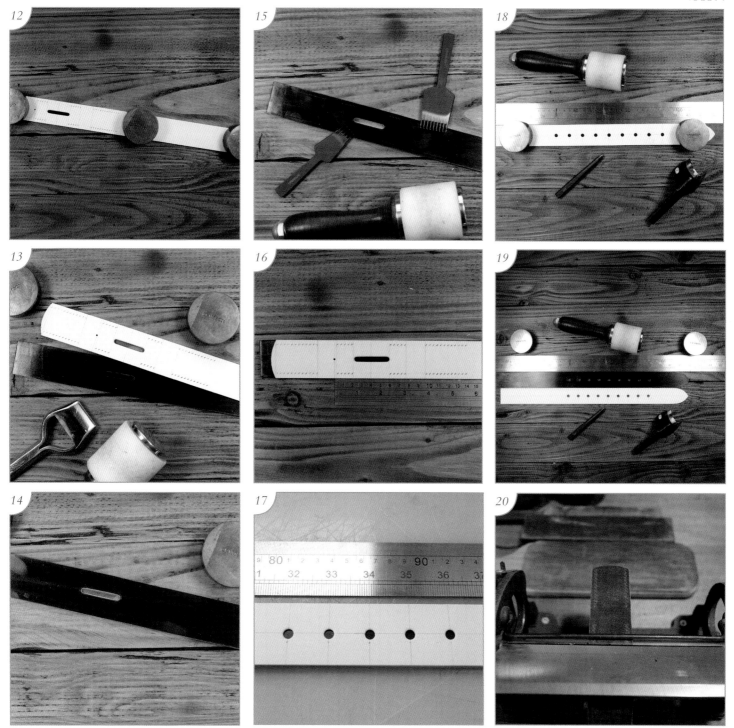

12

13

14

15

16

17

18

19

20

21 Skiving makes it easier to bend the strap and stitch it and also makes it more comfortable to wear.

If are not confident, leave it for now. A skiving knife or splitter is the ideal tool for this job, but I appreciate these may be skills you will want to work up to first.

22 Once the strap is cut to length, all holes have been made, and you have thinned down the back (if you are going to), the next task is to dress the belt. A crease is a nice way to finish the edges, but if you are using bridle leather, the creasing iron will need to be hot.

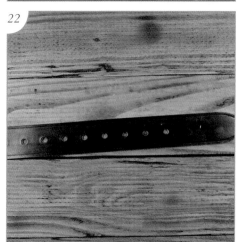

23 Ensure you have had a good practice with the tool first before applying a crease to the edge of the leather. Once creased, bevel all the edges for a nice finish.

24 Apply whichever solution you prefer to slick the edges down. I will use Tokenol. Slick until a nice even sheen has been achieved, then lightly sand and apply Edge Kote and beeswax and slick again.

25 You are now ready to stitch the buckle into the strap.

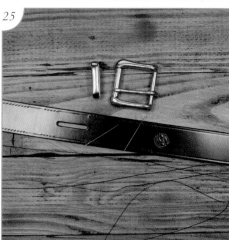

26 Put the buckle in place, ensuring it is the right way around, and fold the leather around it.

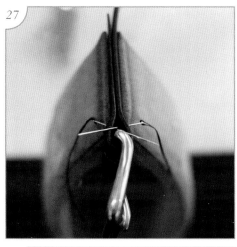

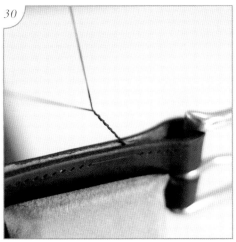

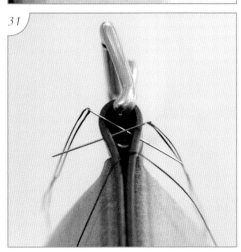

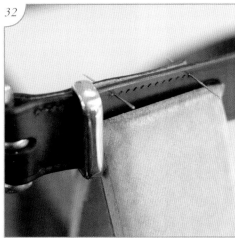

27 Now you can start stitching. It's best to stitch toward the buckle in this instance. Start the third hole back in the row of five holes, ready for your two backstitches.

There are five holes, so there will be only four stitches. Stitch to the fourth hole only.

Once you have stitched to the fourth hole, put the front needle into the fifth hole but make it come out between the two pieces of leather.

28 Do the same for the back needle. Now, with both needles sitting between the two pieces of leather, pass the needles through to the other side, ensuring you do not get tangled in the buckle.

29 Now turn the piece over in the clam.

30 Twist the two threads together twenty times or so.

31 Take one of the needles and pass it through the first hole from the inside out to the front of the leather and then do the same with the second needle to the back.

32 In this position, you can now continue stitching, finishing off with two backstitches.

Once the buckle has been stitched in, apply the keep.

33 You can now stitch the rows of twelve holes in the same way. Stitch toward the keep, pass the needles through to the middle and through to the other side, twist, turn, take the needles from inside to out, and continue stitching.

Once you have completed stitching in the keep, the belt is complete. Step back and admire your handiwork.

33a

33b

33c

ADVANCED PROJECTS

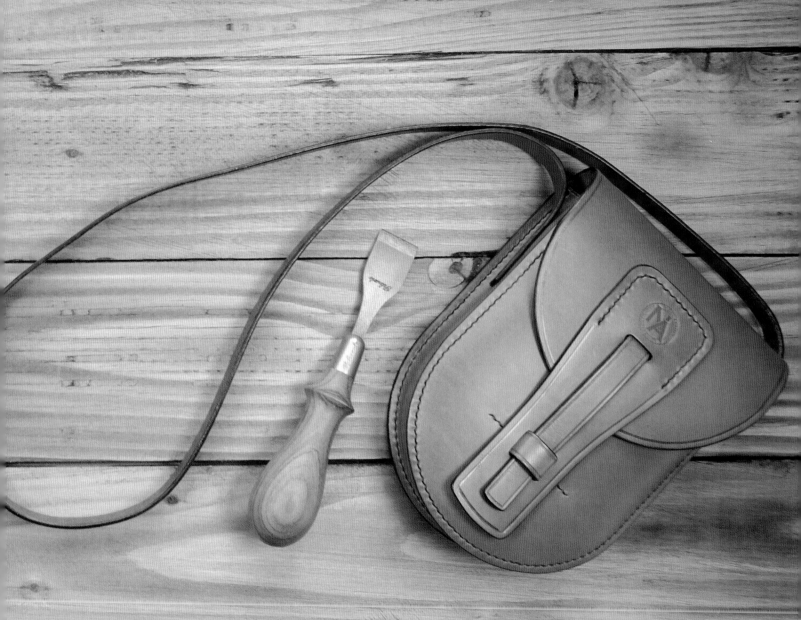

GUSSETLESS BAG

Nearly all bags have some form of gusset—it's what separates the front from the back to give much-needed volume. There are, of course, exceptions, such as molded and tote bags, duffels, and sacks. This is one of those exceptions. In essence, it's a bag made of two parts with a single seam of stitching. We can, of course, add extra bits—straps, loops, and closures—but the body remains, simply, two parts.

TOOLS & MATERIALS

Card for template	Sam Browne stud—
Rule	small or snap
Square	Snap-setting tool
Dividers	Corner cutter, washer, or
Stitching or pricking	coin
irons—7 spi	Needles—no. 4
Pulling block	Thread—0.6 mm
Maul or hammer	Stitching clam
Hole punch—2.5 mm	Scissors or snips
Pippin punch or 3 mm	Crease
hole punch and knife	Edge Kote
Edger (beveler)	Beeswax
Slicker	

Case shoulder, 7–8 oz. (3 mm)

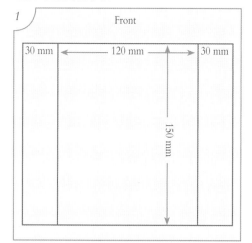

1

Front

30 mm | ← 120 mm → | 30 mm

150 mm

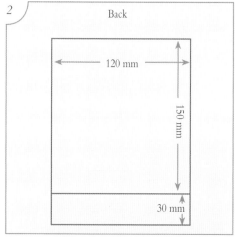

2

Back

120 mm

150 mm

30 mm

3

1 It's the clever measuring and cutting that makes this bag possible. The depth of the bag—what gives the volume—is created by extending the width of the front piece to give the sides, and the length of the back piece to give the bottom.

Curving the corners allows the leather to bend in such a way that when it is stitched, the front is pushed away from the back, thus creating space.

As ever, we need a starting point and a set of dimensions to build on to create the design. The basic size will be 120 mm wide and 150 mm high, and there must also be an idea about depth: 30 mm will do for now. You can play with these figures; this is just a starting point.

Start with the front. At the moment, the design is just a rectangle, 120 mm wide and 150 mm high.

The front will bend at either side to form the sides, and since the depth has been set at 30 mm, you must add 30 mm to either side.

The template for the front of this piece, therefore, is 180 x 150 mm.

2 The back works in a very similar fashion. The sides are taken care of by the front, so the width is 120 mm. It's the bottom to which leather needs to be added, and, again, this is 30 mm.

I'm sure you can begin to see the simplicity of this design and its scope.

3 The remaining calculation is how much leather to add to the back for the flap.

The depth of the bag will be 30 mm or thereabouts, and since the leather has to bend as it goes over the top, you have to allow for this as well. It will not bend in a perfect arc, and you don't want it to, but bend it must.

4 Adding an extra 10 mm will give the leather more space to go from the back to the front in a gentle curve. This gives a figure of 40 mm.

The next decision is where the flap should sit on the front.

Knowing what closure is intended helps with this. Rather than show a metal clasp you may have difficulty in finding, I've gone for a leather tab and a Sam Browne stud.

If you can't find a Sam Browne stud, which would be unusual, a snap will do the same job.

5 The tab is planned to be 115 mm long, with 55 mm of it sitting on the flap, with the top 35 mm being stitched.

I don't want the tab to go up onto the bend, so I have made the flap 60 mm long; the tab will sit on the front, nice and flat.

Adding all of this together gives the back piece the dimensions shown in the sketch:

Bottom	30 mm
Back	150 mm
Flap bend	40 mm
Flap front	60 mm
Total	**280 mm**

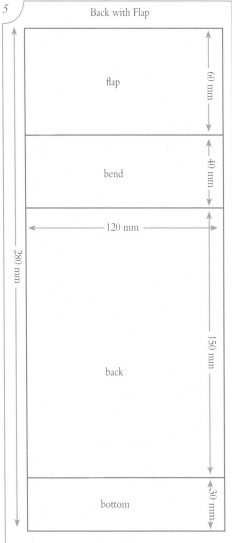

Back with Flap

flap — 60 mm

bend — 40 mm

120 mm

back — 150 mm

280 mm

bottom — 30 mm

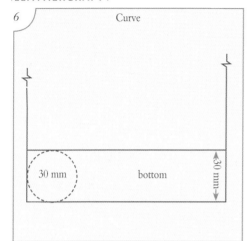

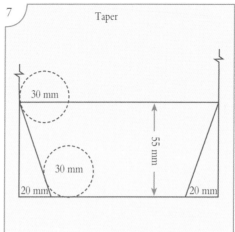

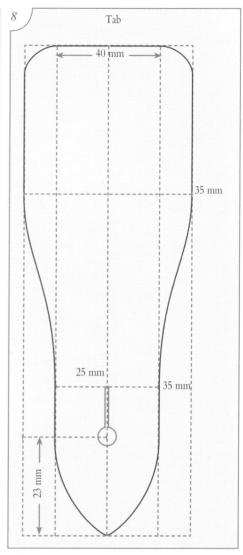

6 For the bag to work, the corners at the base of the back and front pieces need to be rounded, but we have to find the right balance: the bigger the curve, the easier it will be to stitch. However, make them too big and the front curve will encroach into the back curve, and the bag will distort.

The radius of the curve can be no bigger than 50 percent of the depth measurement—in our case 15 mm, so a 30 mm disk would be an ideal choice for cutting the curves.

Make your bag bigger and you can have bigger curves.

7 Dressing the flap is very much a personal choice. I think the tapered cut lends itself well to a design like this. Here I shall cover how to measure and produce mine, but you can experiment with yours.

Mark 55 mm from the end of the flap—this is where the top of the tab will sit—and draw a line.

Then make a mark 20 mm in from each edge and draw a line from this 20 mm mark to the edge of the card at the 55 mm mark. This is the cut for the taper.

The corners will be rounded with the 30 mm disk.

8 Finally, the tab is 115 mm long and 40 mm wide, tapering to 25 mm with an English point at the tip. The taper starts 35 mm from the end and stops 35 mm from the tip, transitioning from the widest point to the narrowest. To make the hole and slot for the Sam Browne stud, I used a pippin punch, but a hole punch and knife make the same slot.

9 I've calculated quite accurately where the tab is going to sit: in line with the top of the front section. In view of this, the center of the hole will be 92 mm from the top of the tab.

Therefore, we know we can add a hole to the front section 92 mm from the top on the center line for our stud or snap. Add this mark to your front template.

10 As a final design choice, I'm adding a scallop to the opening of the bag. I've marked 55 mm from either side of the front section and used a 100 mm disk to cut a curve.

This is very much a personal choice, but I think it adds a nice touch.

11 Now that all the measurements are at hand, you can start to create templates. Using a stiff card, cut the front to 180 x 150 mm, rounding the corners and adding the scallop (if wanted); draw in a center line and add the 92 mm mark for the stud.

12 Next, cut the back piece, 120 x 280 mm, with the taper for the flap, the corners rounded, and a center line.

13 Finally, the tab. Follow the dimensions and cut a template to suit. Again, the style of closure is something you can change to whatever you want; this is just one option. For example, a buckle also works really well with this bag.

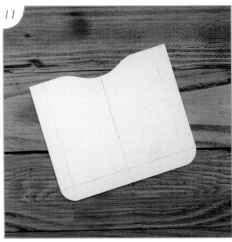

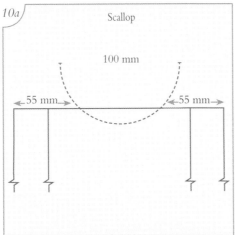

10a

Scallop

100 mm

←— 55 mm —→   ←— 55 mm —→

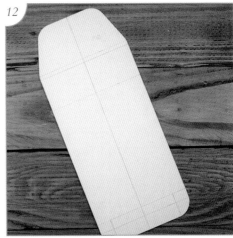

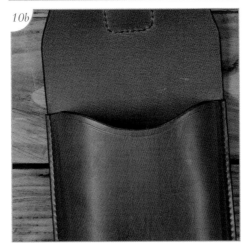

10b

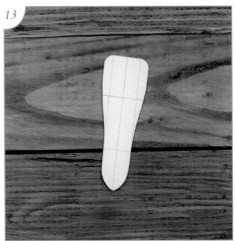

14 With the templates cut, the next step is to work out how to put it together. The bag is stitched on all sides with a single seam: this seam pulls the leather in different directions as you go, and at various points it will look a little odd, but don't be too concerned. The technique we are using is a sound one.

Use a 4 mm stitch line and add this stitch line to the front template.

Next, starting at the center point at the bottom, start making the holes—out and up to the left, then out and up to the right.

If you want to add way lines, do so. It's always a good idea.

15 Having made your holes, count them, then count them again. Once you are happy with the count—I have 115 using a 7 spi iron—add exactly the same number of holes to the back in exactly the same way. Ignoring the center hole in the count, I have fifty-seven to the left and fifty-seven to the right—so with the center hole, this makes up a total of 115.

If you repeat this process on the back, this cannot help but work.

Do it like this first, because using this double-pricking technique helps make the stitching look good; second, it is stitching by numbers, so if the count is correct and you start stitching hole 1 to hole 1, you should finish by stitching hole 115 to hole 115.

Finally, there is no other way to accurately measure where the top of the front should sit against the back before we start stitching. This is the main reason I have included this bag in the book, to extol the virtues of the prepricking method.

I digress; meanwhile, back at the ranch . . .

Having gotten your hole count from the front template, add it to the back.

16 There needs to be a row of stitching on the top of the tab, around the two sides, and at the top. Start and stop the stitching above the 35 mm line. This will be more than enough.

As you have done on each template, start with the center hole and work out and down on each side. This will ensure the last two holes are horizontal.

This is a big focus point and draws the eye—if the stitching isn't level, it will be very visible.

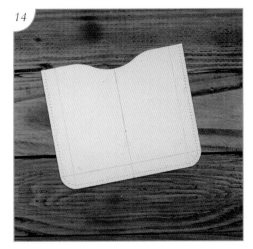

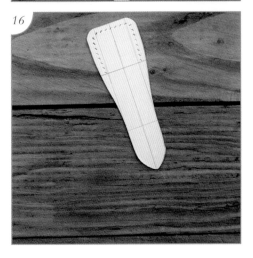

17 Once you have made the holes in the template for the tab, line it up on the flap with the center line and the 55 mm line.

18 In this position, mark the holes through the tab onto the template below. You can transfer these holes through to the leather when you get to the back piece.

19 By now you have had plenty of practice with marking and cutting. Using the templates and all the information on them, cut your leather. I used 3 mm dyed-through shoulder—a firm leather, but not so stiff that it will not bend well at the curves. We want a stiffness to the bag because that is part of the design. Use a leather that will stand up under its own weight to get the effect right.

20 Overlay the template on each respective piece and mark your top holes, center holes, and the holes on each curve, including the tab.

21 Once done, make all of your holes. The stitching at the corners will be testing, since both pieces of leather will try to face different directions, stopping the holes from lining up. Don't be shy with your stitching iron: a little bit of a larger hole than normal will help here. The holes will close up afterward, so give yourself a head start and give that iron a jolly

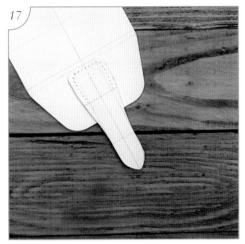

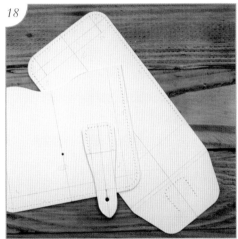

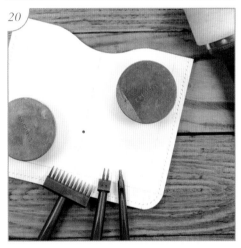

good thump.

With all the holes made, add one extra hole to the end of each row on the back. This is so the stitching goes over the end of the leather at the top to give it a little more support.

22 Having made all the holes, now is the time to dress all the visible edges of the leather: the flap and bend of the back and all of the tab. This will be difficult to do when the bag is made, so sort them out now.

23 You are ready to stitch, and the first order of business is to stitch the tab to the flap. Having made all the holes beforehand, using the templates, you can be certain that the tab will be stitched in place perfectly straight.

24 Once this is done, you are ready to stitch the front to the back. At the outset, both pieces of leather are flat and thus are easy to hold in the clam. Start with a couple of backstitches and work your way down to the first curve.

25 As soon as you get to the curve, the leather will want to bend in a way the clam will not allow, so take it out and hold only the front piece in the clam, allowing the back to hang free.

It will also help if you have the leather a little higher in the clam. This will let the leather bend much more freely and begin to take the form it needs to for the bag. You still need to be firm with the leather: make it go where you want it to go, because it will fight you at the corners—the finger protectors in Project 1 will show their true value here.

Continue stitching until you get to the last holes, finishing with the appropriate number of backstitches.

All that is left to do is to give the edges a light sand and dress, and the bag is complete.

Once it's made, I think you will begin to see the scope of this design and how much fun you can have with it.

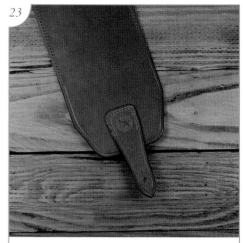

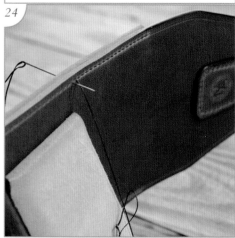

KNIFE SHEATH

In its crudest form, a sheath is three layers of leather—one front, one back, and one sandwiched between. The middle layer—the welt—has had the shape of the knife cut from it so that only the outer sides are left. This is inserted to prevent the edge of the knife, or tool, reaching the stitching. If it did, over time it would cut the stitches, causing the sheath to fail.

Leatherworkers are often asked to make sheaths in one form or another, so this is an ideal way to examine how to add a welt and how to deal with multiple layers of leather—in this case, up to four.

TOOLS & MATERIALS

Card for template	Needles—no. 4
Rule	Thread—0.6 mm
Square	Stitching clam
Dividers	Scissors or snips
Stitching or pricking irons—7 spi	Edger (beveler)
	Slicker
Pulling block	Crease
Maul or hammer	Edge Kote
Large washer or disk	Beeswax
Sanding stick / detail sander	

Bridle shoulder, 7–8 oz. (3 mm)

1 It is very unlikely that you will have the same knife for which I'm making this sheath, so the focus in this project will be on how to measure a knife and how to apply these measurements to a template. I will identify what I did to accommodate my knife. You will need to alter this according to your knife's dimensions.

You can see in the photo on the right how much of the handle is enclosed in the sheath, so we will be adding a welt not only to accommodate the blade and prevent it from cutting the stitching, but also to enlarge the opening to accommodate the handle.

This style of sheath is called a "friction sheath" and is common for shorter knives with little or no cross-guard. The snug fit on the knife in the leather creates grip on the handle. This holds the knife in place, hence the name.

This sheath consists of five pieces of leather:
1. The front
2. The back, which will also form the belt loop
3. The welt
4. + 5. Two welt bolsters for the handle

2 Good measuring is essential for this project. If the sheath is too big, the knife will not be held in place properly. So let's measure the knife. I'm using the dimensions of my knife for the measurements—yours will differ.

Overall length of knife	247 mm
Width of blade	32 mm
Length of blade	130 mm
Thickness of blade	6 mm
Width of guard	36 mm
Thickness of handle	18 mm
Length of handle	117 mm

3 The knife will sit in the sheath with the upper part of the handle exposed. This will put about three-quarters of the knife in the sheath, leaving a quarter exposed to grip.

This is a good ratio for this type of sheath.

4 The maximum width of this knife is 36 mm at the guard. The blade is 32 mm, which is only a 4 mm difference. So to make things easy, I'll work to 36 mm and keep everything inside the sheath straight. This will also make the sheath ambidextrous.

If your knife differs or you are feeling bold, you can step the inside of the welt to suit both the blade and the handle.

If your knife is straight like a bushcraft knife, then simply work to the widest part.

5 The next thing to decide is how wide the welt needs to be. I'm using 7 spi and want the stitching to look strong and bold, so I'm going to bring it farther into the leather and have a 6 mm stitch line.

This will give me more space for a bigger bevel and a rounder edge.

As I am marking my line at 6 mm, I will center this to the welt, so there is 12 mm wide protection to the stitching from both sides.

All this will begin to make the sheath look more robust—which is important when making an item designed for durability and outdoor use.

6 Knowing the welt is to be 12 mm wide and the gap will be 36 mm for the knife, I arrive nicely at 60 mm for the width of our sheath (12 mm + 36 mm + 12 mm).

I can now begin to make the templates.

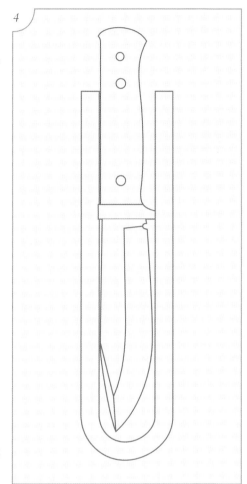

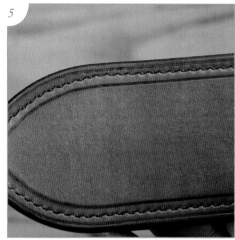

I need two templates—one for the front and one for the back. The welt is a copy of the front, so the same template can be used for both.

While the stitching and shape will be identical for the body of the two templates, the tops differ. The front section will have a curved top, and the back section will be extended to include a strap that will fold back to form the belt loop.

7 This sheath will be ambidextrous, so an English point will help make it symmetrical. This is very much like the belt tip in Project 5, and they would make a nice set if made together.

8 For the first template, start with the front section and cut a piece of card 60 mm wide and at least 250 mm long. Add a center line.

9 Add an English point at one end. For this I used a 100 mm disk as the template.

Mark a point on the center line to cut to; line your disk so that its edge sits against the edge of the card and sits on the marked point. Cut.

Do this on both sides and the point will appear.

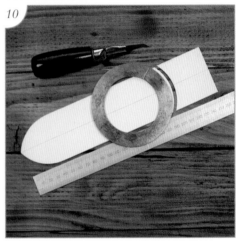

10 The overall length of the front section needs to be 205 mm, so once the point has been cut, measure 195 mm from this point to the top of the card and draw a straight line across the template.

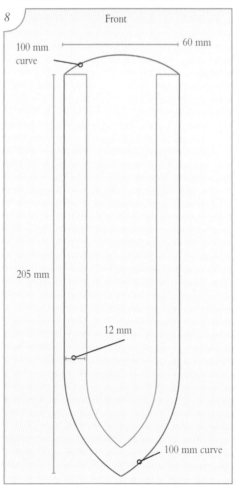

Front

100 mm curve

60 mm

205 mm

12 mm

100 mm curve

11 Cutting the curve above the line will add 10 mm to the length of the sheath, bringing it back to 205 mm.

The same 100 mm disk is used to cut this curve.

To add the curve at the top of the template, place the disk on the line so the curve is above the line. Ensure both the left- and right-hand sides of the curve sit on the line as it leaves the card: this will center the curve. You are ready to cut.

The symmetry of curves is not an obvious detail, but keeping them as close as possible makes the design of the sheath look more consistent.

You are now ready to make the second template. Cut a further strip of card 60 mm wide, but due to the addition of the strap, it will now finish at 365 mm—so cut the card to 400 mm to give yourself plenty of space.

Repeat the process for cutting the point at the bottom of the card.

Lay the first template over the second and mark the top curve—this helps keep everything nicely lined up.

12 Above this line, we will be removing 11 mm of card from both sides. This means we can stitch the strip into place to make the loop and still have space to stitch the sheath together.

Set your rule stop to 11 mm and add a line to either side of the template above the curved line. This is your cut line and will reduce the template to 38 mm wide.

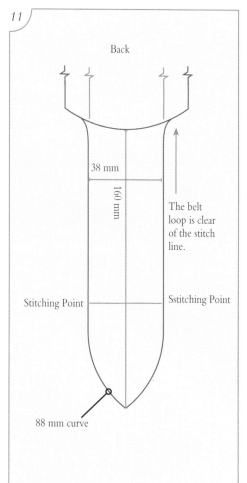

Back

38 mm

160 mm

The belt loop is clear of the stitch line.

Stitching Point

Sstitching Point

88 mm curve

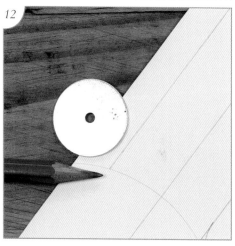

Where this line meets the curve, it needs to curve out so the cut flows naturally and there are no sharp corners.

A smaller disk lined up with the curved and straight line will help with this.

13 The addition of the strap means this template will need to be 365 mm long, so measure from the tip and mark a line at this point.

As before, use a disk to cut the point on the strap end of the template—where your lines cross is your point to cut to.

I am using a smaller 88 mm disk to do this, since it is just a smaller version of the larger cut.

14 With your two templates cut to size, make sure that they fit together neatly; if not, a light sand should resolve any inconsistencies. When you are happy with the match, add a stitch line 6 mm from the edge on the front section only (this section can be used to mark the stitching on all the pieces). At the end of the strap, measure 50 mm from the point and draw a line across the template and add a stitch line.

15 When adding the holes, it is important that the top two holes on the sheath and the top two holes on the strap finish at the same height.

To ensure this happens, start at the center point at the bottom and make your holes in the template, working out and up from this point.

If you have an uneven cut or drift off the line, it will show here—but much better here on the template than on the leather.

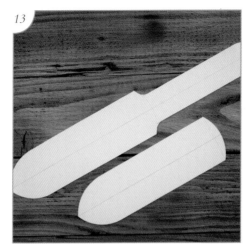

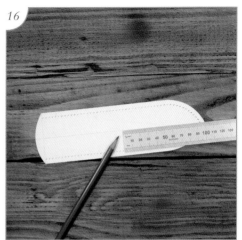

16 There is one final set of holes to be made in the template: we have marked the holes at the end of the strap, but there are no corresponding holes on the back for them to line up against. This strap can be glued in place and the holes made then, but that introduces a bit of guesswork, and that's to be avoided if at all possible.

For the loop to sit correctly, the tip of the strap wants to sit 100 mm from the tip of the sheath. Knowing this, we can take the strap template and lay it over the front template. It is this front template that we will use to mark most of the holes, so it makes sense to put it on here.

Mark 100 mm up from the tip of the front template.

17 Put the strap section of the back template on this mark and line it up to the center line.

18 With this in place, mark all the holes for the strap onto the front section. Remove and make the holes fully.

19 You are now ready to cut the leather. The leather for the front and back will be 3 mm shoulder. The leather for a sheath must not be too thin—if it is, the sheath may bend when it's empty, and then as you replace the knife, it can cut the side of the sheath where it bends.

Try to choose a leather thick enough that the sheath will be quite rigid when it's made.

20 Cut the front and back pieces, using the appropriate templates.

21 The welt needs to be in a thicker leather than the body; my knife is 6 mm thick (yours may differ).

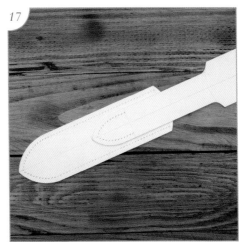

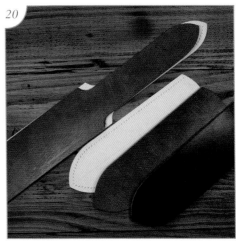

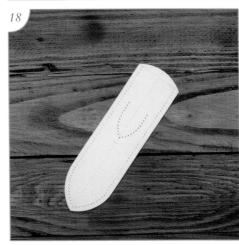

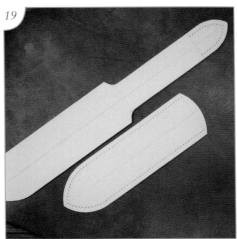

22 I decided to keep my welt cut straight at 36 mm, giving the blade 4 mm of leeway to move.

The choice of leather thickness is important: had I used 6 mm leather, the blade could rattle a little. However, if I chose a 5 mm leather for the welt, the blade would sit better in place—enough to stop the blade moving around, but not so much it would make the sheath hard to use.

23 Cut a section out of the welt leather to match the front section.

24 In addition to the welt piece, two further strips of 5 mm leather will be needed for the top of the welt to open the sheath a little more.

The handle is going to sit inside the sheath, so more space is needed. At its thinnest part, the handle is 15 mm thick, and at its thickest, 20 mm.

25 Looking at the knife in profile, we can see it goes from 6 mm to 15 mm and to 20 mm. This loosely forms the shape of a wedge, so that is how to cut the additional welts. They need to be 12 mm wide and about 100 mm long. If you are able, create a long, slim wedge, tapered from the middle to one end.

I have mine a little longer at this point, since they will be cut to size when glued to the back of the welt.

26 Adding this extra welt to either side will bring the space for the knife up to only 10 mm; we are relying on the leather forming around the handle to accommodate the rest.

This is where friction comes into play to keep the knife in the sheath. With a little pressure and warmth applied to the leather, it will begin to mold to the shape of the handle.

Wetting the leather also helps speed up the process, but for now I'm using conditioner and a bit of pressure.

27 With all the leather pieces cut, we need to ensure they are of a consistent shape and size—put them together to check that this is the case.

This will tell you if your cutting skills are good or need work.

28 Time to begin preparing the leather. Add a 6 mm stitch line to the areas for marking and making holes—the front, back, end of strap, and welts.

Place the template over each section in turn and mark the center hole, top two holes, and several holes along the line. These will act as way points to ensure you are not running off line.

Don't forget to add the strap holes to the back section as well.

Ensure the iron is vertical and that the template is properly lined up, since any variation will put the marks in the wrong place.

If you do have any misalignment, always defer back to the line.

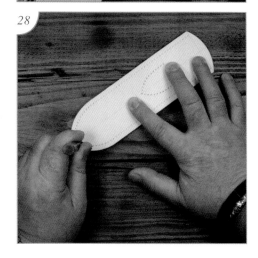

29 Now make all the holes in the leather. You will be going through a number of leather layers when stitching, so to help with this, go a little deeper when making the holes in the welt—this makes the holes bigger and easier to stitch. The holes in the welt will not be seen, so the bigger holes are hidden and will close up over time.

30 You will be stitching a total of 16 mm of leather, so more care now means less frustration later. Take your time, be accurate, and all the holes *will* line up.

For the two short welt pieces, the tops need to be finished to follow the shape of the curve, and the holes need to be added.

A very accurate way of doing this is to glue them in place to the back of the welt section. Do this once the holes have been made in the welt. A little bit of PVA glue will be ideal, since these will be separated once the holes have been marked. You will not be able to punch through both pieces together, so once marked, take them apart and punch the holes in the welt pieces separately.

31 An ideal time to trim and shape the top of the welt pieces is while they are glued in place. They need to follow the same line as the top of the front section.

32 Once trimmed, mark the holes in the welt pieces with a perfectly vertical iron by going through the holes in the welt.

If you have difficulty keeping the irons vertical, use something with a good right angle to assist you—here I'm using the pulling block to keep my irons straight.

33 You can now separate the welt sections and fully make all the holes nice and deeply.

34 At this point, we need to cut the center section out of the welt. Set your dividers to 12 mm (the width decided for this welt) and run a line around the outside of the welt.

Put the rule over this to ensure you have the correct measurement: 12 mm–36 mm–2 mm.

35 When you're satisfied with this line, cut the middle out. You can do this freehand or use a rule and disks if you prefer.

36 Once all the holes have been made on the front, back, welt, and welt sections, and the welt has been cut, it is time to dress all edges that are not being stitched or cannot be dressed once the sheath is stitched.

This will be the top of the front piece, the tops of the welt, and welt pieces, along with the strap that will form the loop.

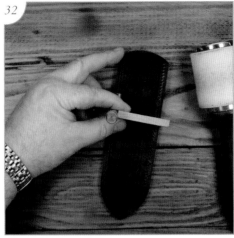

32

35

33

36

34

37 You are now in a position to begin to stitch the sheath together.

First, the strap needs attaching to the back of the sheath to form the loop.

With your holes already made, line up the holes in both parts with a couple of needles. Place in the clam and stitch.

Once this is done, everything else is ready to bring together.

If you are satisfied that all your holes are positioned correctly, the pieces can be glued together. If you are not confident and feel you may need a little flexibility, don't glue.

One of the easiest ways to line everything up is to use a needle through the first hole of each piece and a further needle in another hole toward the end of the tapered welt section. This will hold the front, welt, welt section, and back together while you place it in the clam.

With the needles sitting at a nice right angle, place everything into the clam.

It will be tricky to get the sheath to sit in the clam centrally, since the loop will be in the way, so a little flexibility is needed.

38 It may help to replace the cutout from the welt back into the sheath to stop the leather being bent too much by the clam. You are now ready to begin stitching.

All the holes have been made, so the stitching will look good both on the front and the back, and there is no reason to worry about uneven stitch lines. You can focus on the stitching.

However, you may find it difficult to get the needles through. If you do, a "soft" awl can be used—this is an awl blade that has had all the sharp edges and point polished off. It is like the needles, blunt. You can't buy this; instead you have to make one.

This soft awl will not cut new holes, but it will line up the holes you've made and open them up a little to make stitching easier.

39 This is, by far, a lengthier process than the traditional method of making a sheath, but it will ensure far more accuracy for those new to leatherwork and still finding their feet. It will also make certain that the stitching on both the front and back is very consistent.

Once stitched, give the edges a light sand, then bevel and dress them. Because there are so many layers, you may need to do it several times to get a nice, clean edge.

I am using a larger edger (or beveler) to give the edges a rounder feel and make the black edge a little stronger visually— again adding to the robust message we are trying to deliver.

To finish, insert the knife and apply a liberal amount of conditioner to the leather with a clean cloth.

Rub this in firmly around the handle of the knife and you will see the leather begin to take on its new form.

Your sheath is now ready for use.

DICE CUP

Stitching cylinders in leather is a true test of your skills. You will need to use an awl, and your measuring and cutting have to be at their absolute best: precision is the key. A dice cup is the perfect way to learn the process for stitching round boxes and tubs.

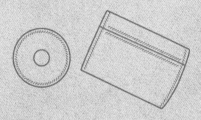

TOOLS & MATERIALS

Rule	Saddler's awl
Square	Stitching form—
Dividers	67 mm round
Stitching or pricking	Scissors or snips
irons—7 spi	Edger (beveler)
Pulling block	Slicker
Maul or hammer	Crease
Needles—no. 4	Edge Kote
Thread—0.6 mm	Beeswax

Case shoulder, 8–9 oz. (3.5 mm)

1 We are working to the size of the form, so the internal measurements are used to dictate the size of the cup. The cup will be lined, and how we do this is a little different from the way we would use the lining to act as a lip for a lid.

One thing you do need for this project is a round form that can be held still, so the item can be held steady for stitching. Here I have a 67 mm plastic rod, 130 mm long, and another at 62 mm wide: both can be held in a carver's vice.

2 It is very hard to make a pattern for a round item like this, so this is one of those projects that is built on the go. Card won't bend, and if you use paper it will not give us a true measurement, since the thickness of the leather affects how it travels around a form.

In view of this, unless you are adding hardware or a design to the item, a template will not be of much use.

We do, however, need a starting point. You know you are building your cup onto a 67 mm round form. The equation for working out the circumference of a circle, remembering your school days, is to multiply the diameter (67 mm) by pi —which is 3.14159265359 . . . and a whole string of other numbers—which gives the figure of 210.38 mm

This would be accurate if the material you were wrapping around the form were flat like cloth or paper, but leather is thicker, so you have to add that thickness into the equation.

First, shorten pi to 3.14 for ease and add the thickness of the leather. In this case it is 3.5 mm, so your equation looks like this:

Diameter of form	67 mm
Thickness of leather	+ 3.5 mm
Pi	x 3.14
Total	**221.37 mm**

If your form or the thickness of your leather differs, adjust the numbers as needed.

You have the width of the leather, but now you need the height—this is the full height of the cup—and this will finish at 100 mm.

This piece is now ready to cut; working to the measurements, cut a piece of 3.5 mm thick leather, 221.37 mm wide and 100 mm high.

On the long cuts, cut the leather straight; on the ends for the butted seam, undercut them a little. The idea is to give a little bit of space at the back of the leather to allow the front to meet cleanly.

Cut it so you are taking an extra 1 mm off the back. If you cut them straight, it will leave a little gap at the front.

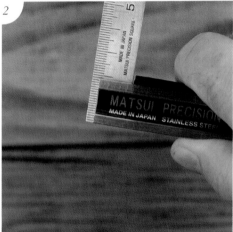

3 This piece will be stitched along the butted seam, where the two edges meet when it is formed into a tube—so these two edges need a 4 mm stitch line.

4 The bottom of the cup will have the round base stitched in place, and at the opening the lining will be stitched to the outer—so both the long edges will also need a 4 mm stitch line.

5 You are beginning to blend stitch lines now, and if you are not careful our stitching will look messy. The top and bottom are, in essence, full circles, so it is best not to disturb them with the stitching along the spine.

In view of this, the stitching of the spine should stop one stitch short of the stitching at the ends.

6 When adding the holes for the butted seam, mark the center of the leather on the stitch line. Also, mark out from this point where the stitching stops short, at the same distance at the top and bottom of the tub.

When marking your holes, punch only about 1 mm into the leather—so just prick your holes.

The stitching will be coming out of the edges of the leather, not the back.

The top row of holes will be going through all the way, so fully mark and make these holes at the top.

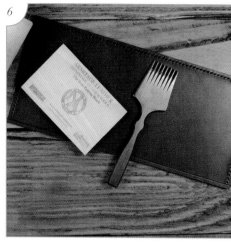

7 Finally, the holes in the bottom need making. Again, these holes will be stitched at an angle, and while they are coming out on the back, they will not be in line with the front, so they only need pricking into place.

8 With all the holes made on the outer piece, you need to do a little more work to the holes for the butted seam. Each hole will come out on the edge of the leather just below halfway.

9 Using a fine awl, push through from the hole on the surface to the edge of the leather, trying to get the blade to come out just below the middle. Try not to mark the surface of the leather while doing this.

This will take practice, so try the technique on a piece of scrap first. The idea is to get the holes on the left to meet the holes on the right so they line up neatly. No stitching should be visible on the inside.

10 Once the holes have been made, the seam is ready to be stitched together. Put the leather onto the form and hold it in place with several rubber bands.

11 If your holes have been made well, they will begin to line up, but you can use an awl just to encourage this.

Begin stitching your seam, applying sufficient tension to pull the leather together, but remember that the

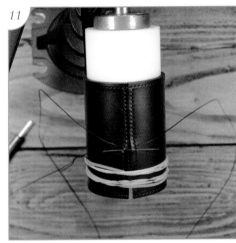

stitching will be pulling at an angle; too much tension and the leather will tear.

12 Once the seam is stitched, you have a tube. Now you're ready to add the next piece—the lining.
 To determine the height of the lining, you need to know the thickness of the base. I am using two 67 mm disks for the base, one in the same leather as the outer and one in the same leather as the lining.

13 For the lining I am using a lighter leather, 2.5 mm in a midbrown.
 I want to attach the lining in such a way that it creates a step for the disks to sit on, which will help keep them in place while stitching.

14 In view of this, my lining needs to be 94 mm high to allow for the thickness of the two disks.
 The width is calculated in a very similar way to the outer leather. This will sit within the original diameter, so the calculation will look like this:

Diameter of form	67 mm
Thickness of leather	2.5 mm
Pi	x 3.14
Total	**202.53 mm**

You can see that the thickness of the leather has now been removed to get the measurement.
 This piece now needs to be 202.53 x 94 mm.

Again, it will need the ends cutting at an angle so they fit together. It is much harder to overcut, so cut this piece from the back and slightly undercut.

15 Test the lining in your tube to make sure it fits. Once you are happy with the lining, glue it into place with some PVA, but make sure it is level with the top and that you have your 6 mm gap at the bottom for the disks.
 Place the tube over the 62 mm rod and sew the top row of stitching at the opening. You will need to use your awl for this, since the holes have not been made in the lining. This is where the glue will help. The better bond you have, the easier this will be.
 Once the lining is stitched into place, you will need two disks of leather, one to match the outer and one to match the lining: cut a 67 mm disk from each.
 A simple way to do this is to place the form over the leather and mark around the circumference with a scratch awl and then carefully cut it out.

16 Once the disks are cut, glue them together flesh side to flesh side.

On the outer side, add a 4 mm stitch line and prick a row of holes. As before, these will be stitched at an angle, so go in only about 1 mm.

17 Once all the holes have been marked, use an awl to make the holes. This time, you want the awl to come out a little lower toward where the two disks join. When making the holes, they need to be in line with the center—imagine the spokes of a wheel: every spoke comes from the center and fans out as it reaches the rim—the awl blade needs to do the same.

If the holes are out of line, the holes will be difficult to find with the awl when stitching.

18 With all the holes made, glue the disks into the base of the tube and you have a cup.

19 It's time to stitch the base in. I have used the same iron to make the holes on the outer piece as I have the holes on the disk.

They will not match. If you were to count the holes on each piece, you will have fewer holes on the disc. Don't worry; this is not a problem. Begin stitching the disk in place.

20 Before long, you'll notice that the holes will fall out of line. To remedy this, stitch to the next available hole on the outside, but use

the hole you have just stitched on the disk. No stitch will appear on the disk, but one will appear on the outer and the holes once again line up. Every time your holes fall out of line, lose a stitch by using this technique.

Once it's stitched, you are almost done. All that is left is to dress the edges; no crease is needed, just a nice. clean bevel edge, a slick coat, and burnish.

Time for a game, or even some pencils.

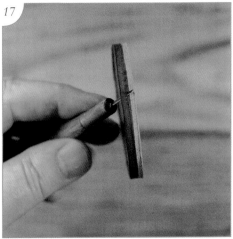

ROUND-BOTTOM BAG

This is an excellent project for budding bag makers since it adds a gusset—with all the scope that can bring. Breaking down the construction of a bag to its most basic component parts, we have the front, the back, which includes the flap, the gusset, and the strap.

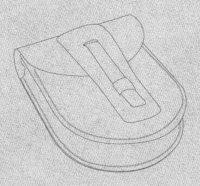

TOOLS & MATERIALS

Card for template	Skiving knife
Rule	Leather chisel
Square	Needles—no. 4
Dividers	Thread—0.6 mm
Stitching or pricking irons—7 spi	Stitching clam
	Scissors or snips
Pulling block	Edger (beveler)
Maul or hammer	Slicker
Crew/oblong punch—15 mm	Crease
	Edge Kote
Disk—125 mm	Beeswax

Case shoulder, 6–7 oz. (2.5 mm)

1 The size of the bag at this time is irrelevant—it can be any size you want it to be. I have chosen a set of dimensions and kept them small so the project is achievable, but once you understand the process, you can make it to any size and shape you want. We will be focusing on how it all goes together.

The gusset is a strip of leather that separates the front from the back to give the bag its space. The simplest way to attach a gusset is two simple seams, one front and one back. This will form a C-shaped gusset.

While there are a multitude of ways to make this bag, I will keep it simple. Get the foundation under you, and you have something to build on.

The design I have chosen is a modern take on an old English horseshoe pouch, which originally attached to saddles to contain spare horseshoes for long journeys.

The interesting thing about this pouch is that there is no hardware; it is all leather and stitching.

I am adding a stitched strap set to a length, but if you want you can always add a buckle to make it adjustable.

2 We are going to skip the C-shaped gusset and go straight to an S-shaped gusset.

3 This is where the front seam is a lapped seam, with the front overlapping the gusset rather than sitting next to it. This causes the gusset and

front to bend out, giving the bag a slight swell.

The back seam is kept as a simple seam; this forces the gusset to bend back in, causing it to form the S shape.

This is just one of many options when adding gussets.

The size of the bag is going to be 125 mm wide and 165 mm high—dimensions I have chosen to keep it small. It's better to start with a scaled-down version for practice—less leather is being used, so if you make a mistake it is less costly, and it takes less time to build. When starting out, it is unrealistic to expect a new project to work the first time. Once you have a good command of the techniques needed, adjust the size or shape to what you want, and do it again. This is one of the joys of leatherwork: you are limited only by your imagination.

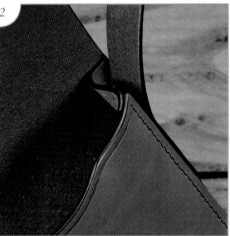

Adding a gusset can present a lot of problems, measuring it to the right size being the biggest.

Traditionally, the part of the body we are working on has had the holes pricked; the gusset is then glued into place, trimmed, and stitched using an awl.

This technique works well and is a sound way of making a bag. The issue comes if you are not adept with an awl.

It takes a very long time to learn how to stitch proficiently with an awl to get your stitching looking good on both the front and the back. This can be very frustrating and can become quite a hurdle. In view of this, we will be

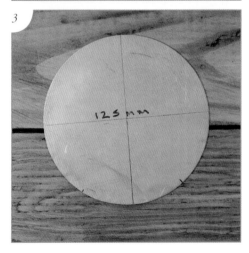

prepricking all of our holes and counting them, bringing a level of precision to your work.

If you take only one thing away from this book, take this. It will get you out of a lot of difficult spots and increase the quality of your stitching very quickly.

To begin, the bottom of the bag and the end of the flap will be rounded. I have a 125 mm disk that I use to cut around.

4 If you have something similar, use it and adjust the dimensions to suit. For example, a CD is 120 mm, so if you use one of those, your bag will be 120 x 165 mm—use what you have; the size at this point is not important.

The 125 x 165 mm dimension is the size of the front piece; now we need to calculate the size of the back.

To do this we need to know two things: the width of the gusset and how far down we want the flap to come on the front of the bag.

First, the gusset. There is no hard-and-fast rule for how big this needs to be; the volume you want and the size of the bag have an impact, but we have to start somewhere, and I have chosen 30 mm. I will be using a stitch line of 4 mm and a 1 mm allowance for the leather to bend—this needs adding to both sides to the piece of leather—so the measurement becomes 4 mm + 1 mm + 30 mm + 1 mm + 4 mm = 40 mm.

As for the flap, one-third or two-thirds of the height of the bag are good options, but the hardware we use has an impact on this.

I am using a loop-and-tab system that needs quite a bit of space, so I'm going to bring the flap down to halfway, 82.5 mm—we'll call this 82 mm.

Now that we know the size of the gusset, we can work out how much leather to add for the bend over the top of the bag.

We know the depth will be 30 mm, but the leather will not bend at a right angle; it will arc gently over the top.

This is very much dependant on the stiffness of the leather, and sometimes you have to use trial and error: try bending a piece around to judge how it bends, but for something of this size, one-third the depth of the bag usually works—10 mm.

Knowing these measurements, we can now say that our back piece needs to be 125 x 287 mm (as shown in the diagram at right).

We don't yet know the length of the gusset, but this will be dictated by the hole count. We do know by measuring around the outside of the front piece how long it needs to be.

Cut out the template and measure around the outside with a tailor's tape.

Suffice it to say that we need our gusset to be at least 410 mm long, and we can trim once we have made our holes.

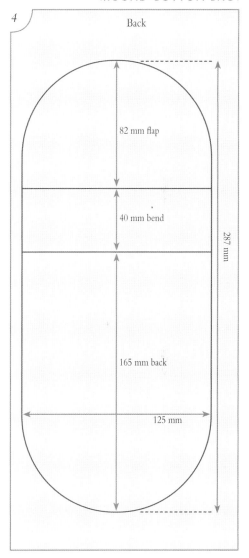

5 The last thing to work out is the looped tab. This is a nice inexpensive closure since you can make it any size to fit any bag. It is a tapered tab, stitched to the flap, and toward the bottom it has a 20 mm wide, 15 mm high hole.

This hole sits over a loop stitched to the front of the bag, and a 15 mm strap slips into this loop, locking it all neatly into place.

The diagram (**5b**) gives the dimensions of the looped tab, and I will explain the placement shortly.

6 We are now ready to cut the templates. This is the cutting list:

Back: 125 x 287 mm
         rounded at both ends

Front: 125 x 165 mm
         rounded at the base

Tab: 50 x 140 mm
         tapered to 40 mm and rounded

Gusset: 40 x 100 mm

There are other parts to the bag that do not need templates; these are

Short strap: 15 x 128 mm
                rounded at one end

Loop: 15 x 100 mm

Shoulder strap: 15 x 1,200 mm

We will come back to these, so for now cut all your templates as rectangles, but don't round just yet. We have a few lines to add, and these will be better done while whole.

7 There are a number of measurements that we need to add to each template as we go to ensure a good fit.

Starting with the back template, add a center line and measure 70 mm from one end, then draw a line across—this will be the flap end. This marks where the top of the tab will sit.

Mark a line 165 mm from the other end. This represents where the gusset will sit.

Now round both ends and add a 4 mm stitch line.

8 For the front template, start by adding a central line. I'm also adding a scallop to the front. I've marked 30 mm in from the left and right on the top and used the 125 mm disk to drawn a curve to indicate where to cut.

9 You need to add three lines measured from the bottom of the template, marked at 45 mm, 52.5 mm, and 60 mm—the top line, stitch line, and bottom line. These indicate where the loop for the closure and the hole on the tab will sit.

Next, set your rule stop back to 52.5 mm and mark two further lines from either edge of the card. This is the outer edge of the hole and where you will

need to set your crew punch to make a slot on either side.

Using a crew punch or hole punch and knife, add two slots on either side of this small rectangle, working inside the lines.

5a

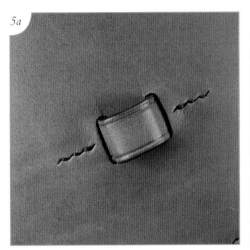

6

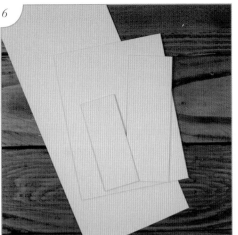

9

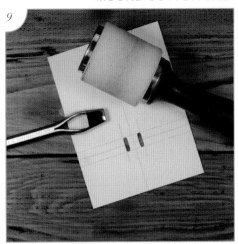

5b

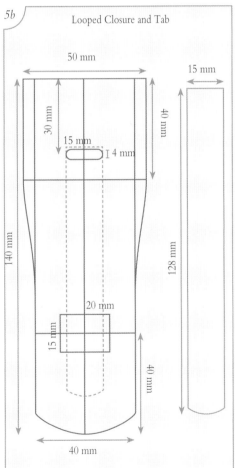

Looped Closure and Tab

50 mm

15 mm

30 mm

40 mm

15 mm

4 mm

140 mm

128 mm

20 mm

15 mm

40 mm

40 mm

7

125 mm

8

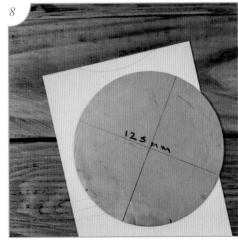

125 mm

10 Finally, round the bottom of the template and add your stitch line. We can add our stitch holes to the template now—I'm sure you are beginning to get used to this by now—start in the center at the bottom, work out and up on both sides, then count your holes. I have ninety-nine holes using 7 spi irons.

While we are still on the front template, we can add the stitch holes for the loop. There will be a single row of stitching in the middle of the strap, four stitches long. Starting one stitch from the outer edge of the small slot, add five holes to the center line on either side.

11 The front template is now complete.

12 On the tab template, add your center line, then add a line 40 mm from each end. Now add a 5 mm line to each side: these are your guides to taper the tab.

It will taper from the top 40 mm line to the bottom 40 mm line.

From the bottom, mark two lines at 32.5 mm and 47.5 mm. These are the top and bottom lines of the hole that needs cutting for the loop.

From the left and right sides, add a line 15 mm in from the edge. These are the left and right lines for the hole.

Now mark a 30 mm line from the top. This is where the slot will be for the strap to sit in.

If you have a maker's mark, this is a good place to add it.

You can adjust the height of this slot to fit your stamp in, if needed.

13 Finally, cut the taper on your template, then round the bottom and the top two corners.

Add a stitch line above the 40 mm mark at the top, and starting from the center, mark and make your holes. We can now place the tab onto the back section, lining it up with the 70 mm line. Center it and mark the holes from the tab onto the back.

We don't really need to add the stitch holes to the back template, since the front has told us everything we need to know.

14 We don't need a full-sized piece of card for the gusset template; this is just for the ends so we can add the stitching for the strap.

This is a row of stitching set 25 mm from the end of the gusset and 35 mm long. It is 9 mm apart, so set your stitch line on the strap to 3 mm.

Cut a piece of card 40 mm wide and 100 mm long and mark your lines and holes.

Count the holes, since this will be the number you add to the ends of the strap. I have ten.

15 That is all the templates cut.

16 We are now ready to cut the leather. Using the templates, cut, mark, and add all holes in the leather that correspond to the holes in the templates.

There are a few extra pieces needed that we don't have templates for.

The leather I am using is 2.5 mm thick shoulder for everything except the gusset. This is in 1.5 mm leather.

Here is the full cutting list again to help:

1. Back   125 x 287 mm
              rounded at both ends

2. Front   125 x 165 mm
              rounded at the base

3. Tab   50 x 140 mm

So far, we have made the holes only for the body on the front section. The template from the front can also be used for marking the back section as well.

Mark the top two holes, the center holes, and a few going around the curve to act as way marks to make sure you do not drift.

In short, we have added ninety-nine holes to our template, so add the same number to both the front and back pieces of leather.

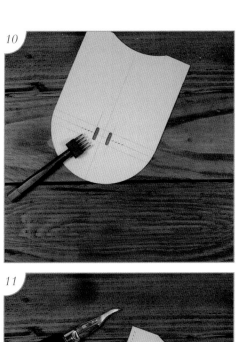

10

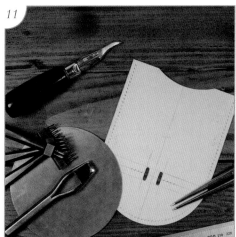

11

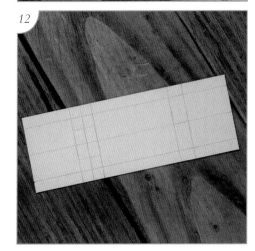

12

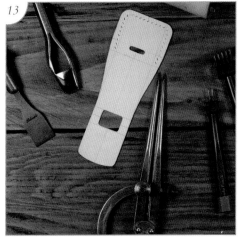

13

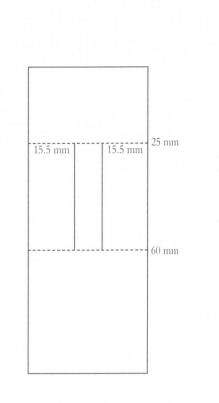

14

Gusset

15.5 mm   15.5 mm   — 25 mm

— 60 mm

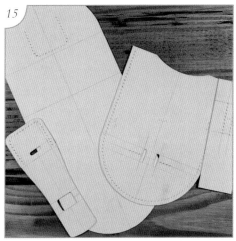

15

16

17 In the same vein, we need to add holes to our gusset. At the moment it is a bit too long, but that is not a problem.

Mark a 4 mm stitch line down both sides and, starting from the same end for both sides, one stitch mark in from the end.

Mark ninety-nine holes (or however many holes your count is), then, very lightly, mark hole 100.

Just inside hole 100 is where we need to cut the gusset. Now cut.

18 The shoulder strap will be 15 mm wide—it only needs to be light for a small bag like this, but it is something you can experiment with.

You will need to add two rows of stitching, each ten holes long, to the strap, as highlighted on the gusset template.

The two rows on the template are 9 mm apart, so set your dividers to 3 mm to allow for this.

19 With all pieces cut and marked, and holes made where appropriate, we need to dress the edges that will not be stitched. These will be

• the flap and bend of the back
• all edge of the front
• all edges of the tab
• all edges of the short strap
• all edges of the loop
• all edges of the shoulder strap
• one edge and both ends of the gusset

The reason we are dressing one edge of the gusset is that this will be visible inside the bag, and this is the edge that will form the lapped seam.

20 We need to set the short strap in place before the tab is stitched to the flap. The flat end is going to be stitched in with the tab, so this end needs tapering down nice and thin. It can then fitted through the slot and glued into place.

Once glued in place, mark the hole again to ensure the holes go through the short strap.

You may need to touch up the dressing a little if the end of the strap can be seen.

21 With the two slots made on the front of the back, the loop needs to be set in place so there is enough space for the tab to sit over it and the short strap to go through it.

Together, these two pieces are 5 mm thick. so the loop has to sit high enough to allow for this.

The strap that will go through is 15 mm wide—so something 15 mm wide and 6 mm thick, such as a bit of wood, would be ideal—I am using a loop stick.

Bend the leather around the stick on three sides and put the ends into the slots. Then flatten the leather out on the inside.

22 Once flat, mark on the loop where the holes need to go. Once the loop has been marked, it can be removed. The holes can be made in the center of the loop, and then the ends cut to length and skived down, ready for stitching.

Everything is now ready to be stitched.

23 The hard part is behind you; the stitching is now working toward the end of the project. It's all about the preparation. Fail to prepare—prepare to fail. We have spent all this time in preparation, and now it's time to bring it together. First, the tab. Let's stitch this onto the flap.

24 Next, stitch the loop into place on the front.

25 Now we are ready to stitch the front to the gusset. With both pieces of leather grain side up, place the front onto the gusset, with the finished edge placed under the edge of the front.

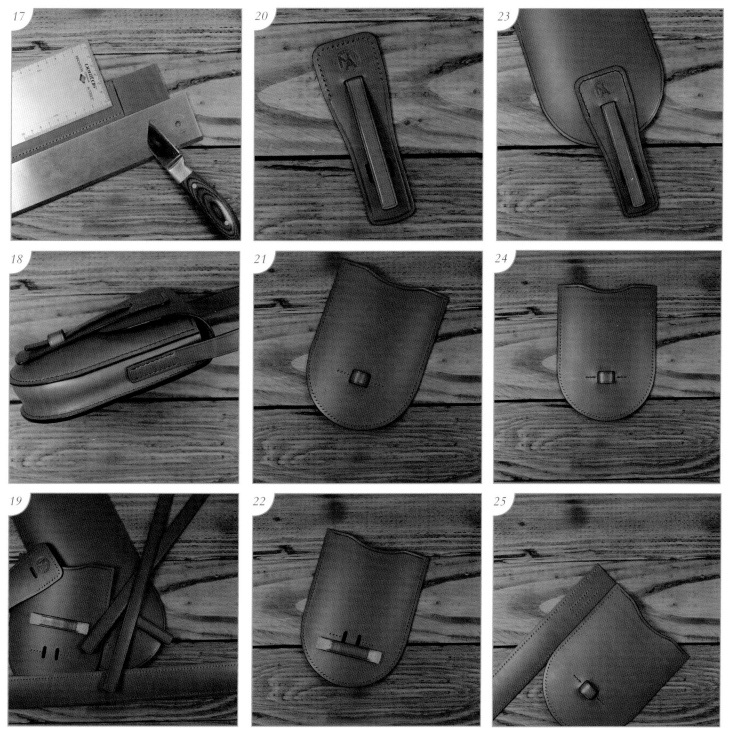

26 This will be a little awkward to get started in the clam, and setting it at an angle will help.

Once you are underway and approaching the curve, place the front in the clam and let the gusset hang free. It will want to bend, so if you let it hang, it can do so.

Once the gusset has been stitched to the front, it is time to add the strap. It will be easier to attach it now, since we can still access the gusset.

27 The front, gusset, and strap are all as one; these now need stitching to the back. At the outset, the front and gusset can be set with the back, flat in the clam.

28 Again, once you get to the curve, keep the back in the clam and let the front and gusset hang. Once this has been stitched, the exposed edge can be dressed.

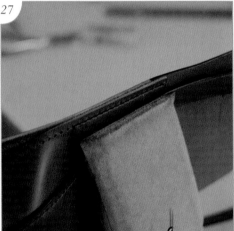

SUPPLIES

The difficulty with providing a suppliers list is that it is particular to me and my location.

By all means, use any information listed below to your full advantage, but don't forget to search locally. I do not know every supplier, and you never know what may be near you.

All suppliers are listed alphabetically, not in order of favor. I describe the item and provide the website; you may have to do a short search.

When speaking with the suppliers, tell them I sent you. They may not give you a discount, but you never know—I might get one . . .

LEATHER

The leather I favor here in the workshop is finished shoulder and bridle butt, and this is what has been used for the projects in this book.

Supplier	Item	Leather	Website
A&A Crack and Sons	Round-Bottom Bag Stitching Iron Pouch	Buttero Tan	www.aacrack.co.uk
Abbey England	Belt	Sedgwicks Bridle Butt, Dark Havana	www.abbeyengland.com
J & FJ Barkers	Knife Sheath	Oak Bark Bridle Tanned Shoulder in Dark Stain	www.jfjbaker.co.uk
LePrevo	Dice Cup	Matt Waxy Dyed through Shoulder	www.leprevo.co.uk
Metropolitan Leather	Slip Pouch	Lyveden, Burnt Tan	www.metropolitanleather.com
	Pocket Protector	Lyveden, Burnt Tan	
	Card Holder	Lamport, Dark Tan	
	Pencil Roll	Lyveden, Burnt Tan	
	Passport Cover	Lamport, Dark Brown	
	Gussetless Bag	Lyveden, Burnt Tan	
	Finger Protectors	Pitsford Pigskin	

HARDWARE

Supplier	Item	Size	Website
Abbey England	West End Swelled Roller Buckle	1½" (38 mm)	www.abbeyengland.com
	Sam Browne Stud	Small	
	Saddler Rivets	14 g	

TOOLS

Supplier	Item	Size / Type	Website
Abbey England	Saddlers Awl	1½"	www.abbeyengland.com
	Saddlers Clam	–	
	Screw Crease	–	
	Rivet Setter	14 g	
	Dividers	6"	
	Crew Punch	Various	
	Bone Folder	8"	
	Strap End Punch	1½" (38 mm)	
	Strap Cutter		
Amy Roke	Irons	8 spi, 3.38 mm	www.atelieramyroke.com
Axminster	Rule	Various	www.axminster.co.uk
	Rule Stop	–	
	Square	150 mm	
	Detailed Sander	4 Pack	
	Carvers Vice		
Barry King	Maul	32 oz. Round	www.barrykingtools.com
Crimson Hide	Irons	7 spi, Japanese, 3.85 mm	www.crimsonhides.com
	Weights	–	
Direct Plastics	Round Nylon Forms	65 mm	www.directplastics.co.uk
George Barnsley	Knife	Clicker	www.georgebarnsleyandsons.co.uk
	Scratch Awl	–	
H Webber & Sons	Snips	TC1	www.hwebber.co.uk
	Splitter	84	
John James	Needles	No. 4 Saddlers Harness	www.jjneedles.com
Just Wood	Slicker	Round and Flat	www.justwood.com
	Pulling Block	Various	
KS Blade Punch	Irons	7 spi, 3.85 mm	www.ksbladepunch.com
	Hole Punch	Various	
Maun	Cutting Edge	Various	www.maunindustries.com
Palosanto	Beveller	1 and 2	www.palosanto-factory.com
	French Skive	12 mm	
Partwell	HY78 Cutting Board	25 mm	www.partwell.com
Terry Knipschield	Knife	Shark	www.knipknives.com/leather.php

DEDICATION

I have pondered this for some time, and the truth of the matter is that this book would have no value without you, so, it is to you that I dedicate this book: to the reader, the student, the leather curious.

It is you who view my videos, who follow me online and come to the workshop for lessons.

It is you whom this book is for. If you did not ask, I would have no reason to tell, so thank you, thank you for your support, thank you for your questions, and thank you for your desire to learn.

ACKNOWLEDGMENTS

I would like to take this opportunity to thank a few people without whom this book may not have made it to the bookshelves.

Stevie Bea. Stevie is my daughter and has the prestigious honour of having taken the cover photo along with a number of others in this book. She has a good eye for detail and a wonderful way of bringing an image to life.

Shaun Bexley. Shaun took the wonderful image of me box stitching which, incidentally, won him a competition.

Jennifer Roberts. Jenny helped with a couple of difficult shots in the book and also drew the lovely dragon featured in the Pencil Roll project.

Emma Francis. Without Emma this book may not have been completed. It was her support and persistence that was the driving force behind this book when it was needed most.

Emma also assisted with many of the photos and ideas for the projects.

Thank you.